The
NEWPORT PICTORIAL

First Edition
1906

Newport
COUNTY BOROUGH

BWRDEISTREF SIROL
Casnewydd

First Published 1906

This edition specially produced
by
Cedric Chivers Limited, Bristol
for the publisher
Newport County Borough Council
Newport Libraries & Information Services
John Frost Square,
Newport NP9 1PA
1998

ISBN 0 907719 17 1

Printed in Great Britain by
J.W.Arrowsmith Ltd., Bristol

PUBLISHED UNDER THE AUSPICES OF THE NEWPORT CORPORATION.

The NEWPORT PICTORIAL

FIRST EDITION

FIRST YEAR OF PUBLICATION

Copyright ENTERED AT STATIONERS HALL

ARCH.H. EDWARDS '05

PRICE 6d.

POSTFREE 9D.

Printed & Published by the Proprietor, W. Jones, Cambrian Printing Works, 159 Commercial Street, Newport. 1906.

COMMERCIAL STREET (SHOWING WESTGATE HOTEL) AND TOWN HALL.

Photo. A. & G. Taylor, Newport.

GENERAL VIEW OF BELLE VUE PARK.

THE NEWPORT PICTORIAL.

To our Readers and the Public.

In placing before the Inhabitants of Newport the **First Annual Issue** of

THE NEWPORT PICTORIAL

the Editor trusts that it will commend itself to their favour and be deemed worthy of their support.

The object sought after in the production of the Work has been to present to the Public one likely to do justice to the great and exceptional advantages which Newport so happily possesses in its Marine, Manufacturing, Commercial and Residential resources and capabilities.

In the literary portion of the Book will be found a necessarily brief, but it is believed interesting sketch of the earlier History of the Town, followed by a description of its modern development and industrial and general progress.

Besides the larger and older Works dealing with the History of Monmouthshire* we are also indebted to the admirable "Handbook" of the County, compiled by Mr. A. Morris, of Newport, a little work which we are glad to understand has secured a deservedly very wide circulation.

In the Illustrated Section appear artistic reproductions of a fine series of Photographs, mostly taken specially for this Work, with some never before published. These, it is believed, present for the first time in any book a

COMPLETE PICTORIAL DESCRIPTION

of the splendid Docks, the more striking architectural features of the Town, and of the beautiful Public Parks (notably Belle Vue and Beechwood), Roads, all of which go to render Newport one of the most attractive, desirable, and advantageous Seaports and Towns in the British Isles.

The Illustrations also of the numerous Places of Public Worship, will, it is believed, be an unfailing source of interest to very many persons aware of, and sympathetic with the important influences radiating therefrom in the promotion of the happiness and well-being of the General Community.

To the Advertisement Section, particular attention is invited.

*Also known as "Gwent," a word having its root in "gwen," a smile; hence "the fair or smiling land" (*vide* Mr. Morris's Handbook).

In carrying out a Work which has necessarily involved much trouble, the Editor has gratefully to acknowledge most kind and valued co-operation from various quarters.

Special thanks are due and are tendered to Mr. John Macaulay, the able and respected Superintendent of the Alexandra Docks and Railway, for his courtesy in granting the use of the splendid Views of the Docks which embellish these pages.

The Editor has also to express grateful acknowledgment to the Town Clerk, Mr. A. A. Newman, for information kindly given; and to several other gentlemen in official positions.

For the admirably selected and well executed Photographs used for the body of the Illustrations, the Editor is indebted to Mr. W. Chalklin, the experienced and at all times courteous Manager of Messrs. A. & G. Taylor, Photographers, Wesley Chambers.

The excellent Typographical features which characterise the Book are entirely due to the initiative, good taste, and technical knowledge of Mr. Arthur S. Flower, Manager of Mr. W. Jones's Cambrian Printing Works, Newport, as is also the original inception of the undertaking, the result being to produce a book that will, we are sure, be cordially welcomed by all classes as one that has long been urgently called for in the highest interests of the Town.

It only remains to add that it is proposed to publish in each succeeding year fresh issues of

THE NEWPORT PICTORIAL,

with such additions and new features as the development of the Town and Docks, under the enlightened rule of the Town Council and Harbour Commissioners respectively, and the enterprise of the inhabitants, may render desirable.

"**The Newport Pictorial**" will thus, it is confidently believed, continue permanently to help forward the Marine, the Manufacturing, and the Commercial prosperity of the Town.

In closing these Prefatory remarks as the sands of the Year of Our Lord, 1905, are running low, the Editor takes this final opportunity of wishing his many kind Helpers and Readers

A HAPPY NEW YEAR!

Newport, Mon.
December, 1905.

A Glance at Mediæval Newport.

EWPORT, to-day the Commercial Capital of the rich and important County of Monmouth, as well as its Shipping Centre, and also for much of South Wales, is distinguished in mediæval history as one of the great strongholds of the Marches, found in those days to be necessary in order to protect the Norman Barons, and their retainers and followers, from the incursions of the brave and warlike natives of Wales. These, the true kinsmen and descendants of the Britons, whom the Romans had dispossessed, had by their daring caused even the conquerors of the gallant Anglo-Saxons to respect their martial prowess, and to take stringent precautions against their advance into the more favoured portions of the adjoining country of England. Thus, Monmouthshire having been over-run, we find that the portions of it bordering upon Wales proper were at an early period placed, by its Norman overlords, under the domination of numerous vast and powerful Castles. Of these we have to-day, in Newport and other parts of the County, numerous grand and historic remains, calculated to make the beholder moralize upon the fleeting and transient character of even the finest and most powerful monuments of human genius and of human ambition.

Gwent (Monmouthshire) claims to be the last district to submit to the arms of Edward I.

OLD NEWPORT CASTLE AND BRIDGE.

From an engraving of Pugh's Picture in Williams's History of Monmouthshire. *Photo, A. & G. Taylor, Newport.*

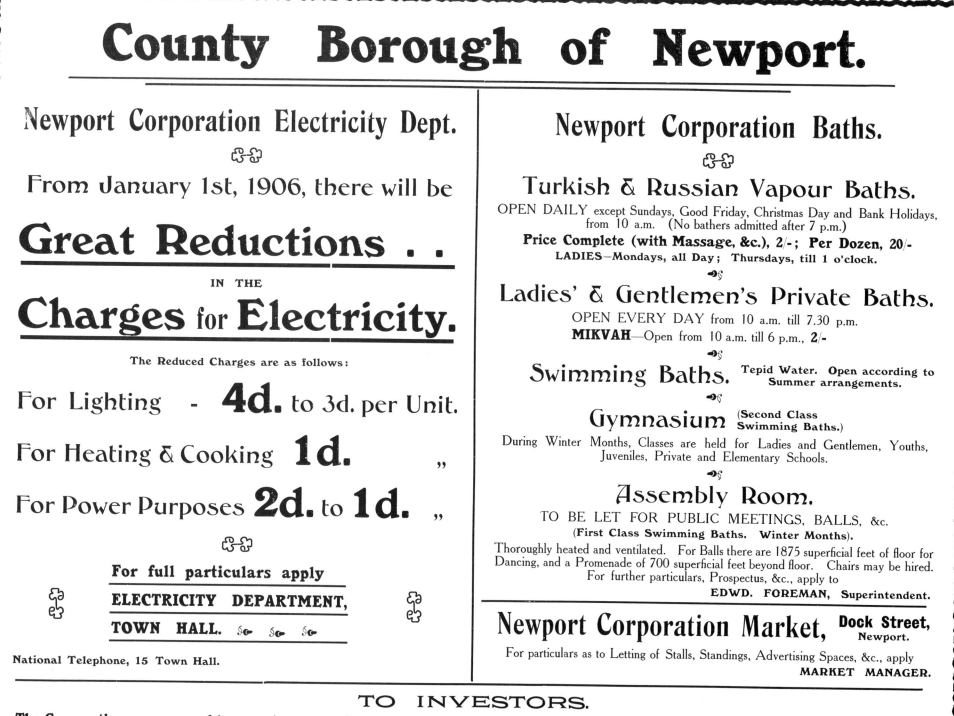

County Borough of Newport.

Newport Corporation Electricity Dept.

❧

From January 1st, 1906, there will be

Great Reductions . .

IN THE

Charges for Electricity.

The Reduced Charges are as follows:

For Lighting - **4d.** to 3d. per Unit.

For Heating & Cooking **1d.** „

For Power Purposes **2d.** to **1d.** „

❧

For full particulars apply

ELECTRICITY DEPARTMENT,

TOWN HALL.

National Telephone, 15 Town Hall.

Newport Corporation Baths.

❧

Turkish & Russian Vapour Baths.

OPEN DAILY except Sundays, Good Friday, Christmas Day and Bank Holidays, from 10 a.m. (No bathers admitted after 7 p.m.)

Price Complete (with Massage, &c.), 2/-; Per Dozen, 20/-
LADIES—Mondays, all Day; Thursdays, till 1 o'clock.

Ladies' & Gentlemen's Private Baths.

OPEN EVERY DAY from 10 a.m. till 7.30 p.m.

MIKVAH—Open from 10 a.m. till 6 p.m., **2/-**

Swimming Baths. Tepid Water. Open according to Summer arrangements.

Gymnasium (Second Class Swimming Baths.)

During Winter Months, Classes are held for Ladies and Gentlemen, Youths, Juveniles, Private and Elementary Schools.

Assembly Room.

TO BE LET FOR PUBLIC MEETINGS, BALLS, &c.

(First Class Swimming Baths. Winter Months).

Thoroughly heated and ventilated. For Balls there are 1875 superficial feet of floor for Dancing, and a Promenade of 700 superficial feet beyond floor. Chairs may be hired. For further particulars, Prospectus, &c., apply to

EDWD. FOREMAN, Superintendent.

Newport Corporation Market, Dock Street, Newport.

For particulars as to Letting of Stalls, Standings, Advertising Spaces, &c., apply

MARKET MANAGER.

TO INVESTORS.

The Corporation are prepared to accept any sum from £20 upwards on deposit, at interest of £3¼ per cent. For further particulars apply
C. CULLUM, Borough Treasurer, Town Hall, Newport.

In the "Secret Memoirs of Monmouthshire," the author glorifies its bravery thus :—

> "To thee, brave Gwent ! praise dost alone belong.
> Thou ne'er wor'st chains, impatient wert of wrong,
> When Saxons, Danes, and Normans, Britain swayed
> Thou scorn'st the servile yoke on others laid,
> With courage great, most bravely did'st maintain
> Thy rights, so long enjoyed ; may they remain ! "

Newport Castle.

One of the most formidable of the great frontier fortresses erected by the Lords of the Welsh Marches was undoubtedly Newport Castle. With this fortress were associated many stirring events in Mediæval, and later British history. In one or another were identified with it such eminent names as those of King William Rufus, Henry I. and II., Robert Fitzroy, the great Earl of Gloucester ; Henry III., and his heroic son, Edward I. The town was visited in 1188, by Baldwin, Archbishop of Canterbury, when preaching the Third Crusade. From hence went the gallant band of men that distinguished themselves at the battle of Crecy, and the siege of Calais. Here was imprisoned, in 1460, the brave Owen Tudor, the grandfather of the victor of Bosworth Field, Henry VII., and thus the founder of the line of our great Tudor Kings and Queens. Charles I. stayed here on his journeyings between Raglan and Cardiff, in the summer of 1645 (after the battle of Naseby). "Charles sought an asylum in South Wales after his defeat. He was entertained right royally at Raglan Castle, and on the 16th of June, 1645, he met the Commissioners for South Wales, at Cardiff. He passed through Newport on that day, when the garrison of 50 men from the Castle came forth to do him honour, under the command of Colonel Richard, Lord Herbert, son of Lord Herbert of Cherbury. At Tredegar House, the 'Iter Carolum' states, that King Charles dined with Sir William Morgan, an ancestor of the present Lord Tredegar. On the 19th of June he returned from Cardiff to Tredegar House, and slept there that night, leaving for Raglan the following day."

Oliver Cromwell, while Newport Castle was being besieged by his forces, stayed in the town; his head-quarters being in the old Elizabethan house in "Church Street," as the Stow Hill thoroughfare was then called. This house at the bottom of the ascent was for long after known as "Cromwell House," and was, unfortunately, pulled down some fifteen years ago.

It must be manifest that a town which possessed so great a stronghold as was Newport Castle when in its prime, which was further defended by stout walls, must have owed them to its highly advantageous natural position on the banks of a noble river, and to its easy defence from attack. It must thus have been in a position to play, and did in fact play, a great part in the history of the country. Nearly eight hundred years with their tempests of nature, of war, and of revolutions, have swept over it since its powerful Norman lords reared its towers and manned its walls with their mailed and armed retainers. It is not surprising that in the passing of those long and tumultuous centuries, during which Monmouthshire shared more or less in every change that swept over England, and bore the brunt of Welsh invasion, civil war, rapine, and fire, and sword, the records of the fortified Town and Castle of Newport should either have entirely disappeared, or their recovery have become the despair of the historian and the antiquary.

Anterior to the Norman period, it may be stated that Newport was the scene of a battle in 918, in which the Welsh, under their chief, the Prince of Glamorgan, after a sanguinary conflict, totally defeated the Saxon Princess or Sovereign, Ethelfleda, Queen of the Mers, the amazon-like daughter of King Alfred. This no doubt was one of the many battles which both during and after the stormy days of the Heptarchy so often desolated the whole country.

Such an event and the importance attaching to the traditional scene of so important an engagement would, with its natural advantages, point out the *Novus Burgus* to the Norman invaders, when they had forced their conquering way so far west, as the proper place at which to establish evidences of their power and a protection to their acquisitions.

Photo, A. & G. Taylor, Newport.

TOWN HALL, DOCK STREET.

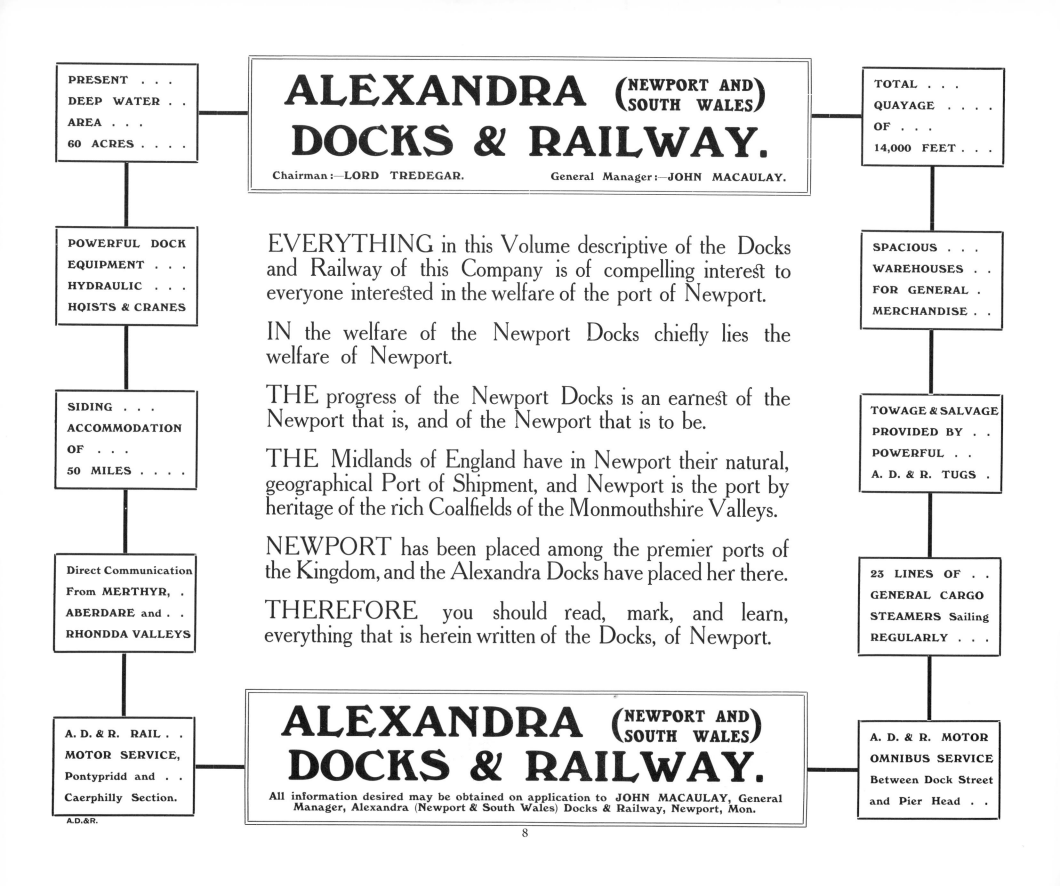

PRESENT . . .
DEEP WATER . .
AREA . . .
60 ACRES . . . .

ALEXANDRA (NEWPORT AND SOUTH WALES) DOCKS & RAILWAY.

Chairman:—LORD TREDEGAR.   General Manager:—JOHN MACAULAY.

TOTAL . . .
QUAYAGE . . . .
OF . . .
14,000 FEET . . .

POWERFUL DOCK
EQUIPMENT . . .
HYDRAULIC . . .
HOISTS & CRANES

EVERYTHING in this Volume descriptive of the Docks and Railway of this Company is of compelling interest to everyone interested in the welfare of the port of Newport.

IN the welfare of the Newport Docks chiefly lies the welfare of Newport.

THE progress of the Newport Docks is an earnest of the Newport that is, and of the Newport that is to be.

THE Midlands of England have in Newport their natural, geographical Port of Shipment, and Newport is the port by heritage of the rich Coalfields of the Monmouthshire Valleys.

NEWPORT has been placed among the premier ports of the Kingdom, and the Alexandra Docks have placed her there.

THEREFORE you should read, mark, and learn, everything that is herein written of the Docks, of Newport.

SPACIOUS . . .
WAREHOUSES . .
FOR GENERAL .
MERCHANDISE . .

SIDING . . .
ACCOMMODATION
OF . . .
50 MILES . . . .

TOWAGE & SALVAGE
PROVIDED BY . .
POWERFUL . .
A. D. & R. TUGS .

Direct Communication
From MERTHYR, .
ABERDARE and . .
RHONDDA VALLEYS

23 LINES OF . .
GENERAL CARGO
STEAMERS Sailing
REGULARLY . . .

A. D. & R. RAIL . .
MOTOR SERVICE,
Pontypridd and . .
Caerphilly Section.

ALEXANDRA (NEWPORT AND SOUTH WALES) DOCKS & RAILWAY.

All information desired may be obtained on application to JOHN MACAULAY, General Manager, Alexandra (Newport & South Wales) Docks & Railway, Newport, Mon.

A. D. & R. MOTOR
OMNIBUS SERVICE
Between Dock Street
and Pier Head . .

A.D.&R.

Origin of "Newport."

The town seems to owe the controlling form of its name to the famous mediæval historian, Giraldus Cambrensis (born 1146),* who, no doubt, while itinerating in these parts with Archbishop Baldwin, describes the town as *Novus Burgus*,—the New Burgh, ville, or town. It is, however, generally agreed that he used this designation, not so much to indicate that the town was then actually "new" or but lately built, as to distinguish it from the adjoining city or town of Caerleon, which though it was even then fast decaying, had been a strong and extensive place in the days of the Romans (to whom it probably owed its existence); and of the Britons before the Saxons and Angles swept over the land, after the Roman retirement; while even the very ruins of that city then excited the wonder and the admiration of the historian who beheld them.

Naturally, however, the inhabitants and natives of the surrounding country did not wait for a writer and historian to give a place of such importance a name. By, and, to them, therefore, it was known as Y Castell Newydd, presumably from the Norman Castle erected at Newport, between A.D. 1130 and A.D. 1140, by Robert, the first Earl of Gloucester.

Photo, A. & G. Taylor, Newport.

THE CASTLE TOWER.

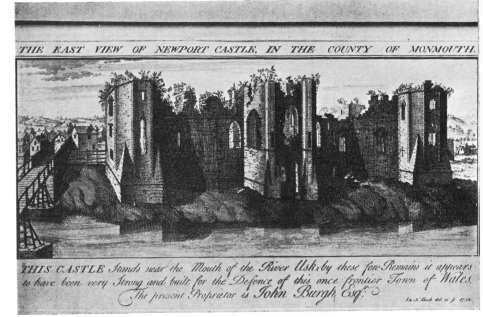

THE EAST VIEW OF NEWPORT CASTLE, IN THE COUNTY OF MONMOUTH.

THIS CASTLE Stands near the Mouth of the River Usk, by these few Remains it appears to have been very Strong and built for the Defence of this once frontier Town of Wales. The present Proprietor is John Burgh, Esqr.

AN OLD VIEW OF NEWPORT CASTLE.

By permission of the Museum and Library Committee.   *Photo, A. & G. Taylor, Newport.*

The Castle played a considerable part in the Barons' War, when the leading barons became suspicious of one another. The famous Simon de Montfort, Earl of Leicester, as the conqueror of Henry the Third and his son Prince Edward (Edward I.), at the battle of Lewes, might have usurped the regal title as he had the regal power, but for the desertion of the Earl of Gloucester, who entered into coalition with the Prince, by which eventually, at the famous battle of Evesham, Leicester's power and his life were both at one blow destroyed.

An Incident of the Barons' War.

In connection with this great struggle between the Barons and the Kingly power, it is interesting to recall that when Leicester was driven out of Usk by Gloucester, after failing in his intention to take possession of Monmouthshire, Leicester entered the Castle of Newport with the intention of falling back by way of the Severn Sea upon Bristowe (as both Channel and city were in old time named), sending thereto for ships to that end. This plan, however, was defeated by the wily Gloucester and the young Prince Edward; for the Bristol boats having been destroyed or driven back, Leicester's army was itself repelled.

* At Manorbeer Castle, Pembrokeshire. His father was William de Barrè, and his mother Angharath, grand-daughter of Rhys ap Theodor, Prince of South Wales. He succeeded his uncle as the Bishop of St. David's, but later, (through some monkish intrigues) resigned; was subsequently re-elected by the Chapter; was objected to by the Archbishop of Canterbury, and this later election nullified by the then Pope. Cambrensis died in 1223.

A. S. MORGAN & Co.,

Telephone, Nat., 228
     „   P.O., 552

Builders, Contractors, Stone Dressers,
Brick Manufacturers, Lime Burners . . **NEWPORT, MON.**

THE NEW ESTATE OFFICES which have been erected by Messrs. A. S. MORGAN & Co., for the RIGHT HON. LORD TREDEGAR, are constructed with local stone and brick walling, faced with Chilmark stone from the Chilmark Quarries near Salisbury, with Chilmark dressings. The buildings are arranged in 4 floors including Basement, which comprises Strong Room, Storage Rooms, &c. The Ground Floor is arranged in 2 divisions, separated by the Central Corridor, one side having the rooms reserved for His Lordship's private use and the Agent's chief room; the other side being fitted up in a similar manner to a bank, and is occupied by the Cashiers and their Clerks. The floor over, generally described as the First Floor, is divided in a similar manner, one division being occupied by the Architect's department, the other division being reserved for special departments.

NEW TREDEGAR ESTATE OFFICE.   *Photo, A. & G. Taylor, Newport*

The Roof, which is of a somewhat high pitch and is covered with boarding, felting and Westmoreland slates with a lead flat apex, is utilised to the full for additional rooms, lighted by broad dormer windows, should the future requirements necessitate further development. The inside woodwork is all executed in teak, which has been finished with linseed oil, and presents a very excellent appearance, the principal feature being the Staircase with its heavy panelled and moulded balustrade, square panelled and sunk newels. The moulded work generally is exceedingly well turned out, the simplicity of the molds used contributing to the general style of finish throughout displayed.

The buildings are warmed with hot water on the low pressure system, and are lit by means of Electricity. The floors are laid with teak on cement concrete supported by steel joists.

Messrs. A. S. MORGAN have also constructed the office desks in the Cashiers' and Architect's departments, also some of the other furniture and cupboards, teak being used for these also.

The Architect is Mr. JOHN F. GROVES, F.R.I.B.A., Architect to the estate.

Messrs. MORGAN have been established since 1892, and have carried out some of the largest public buildings in the town, including the Newport and County Hospital, which elevation is shown on next page; the Newport Infectious Disease Hospital, the Guardians' Offices, the Westgate Chambers; also a large portion of the Newport Tramways, and the entire work of constructing and building the Electric Power Station, Corporation Road. They have also carried out many important contracts for the Great Western Railway, including the latest additions to Newport Station, the New Stations on the Western Valleys, and the New Station at Carmarthen Town, which is the most up-to-date station in South Wales. The firm have also carried out several large Sewerage Contracts in Newport, Cardiff and Rhondda Valley. In addition to the contracting business, they own the Crindau Brickworks, the Undy Stone Quarries which produces a first class building stone, and are also burners of brown and white lime. Their East Usk Stone Works are one of the largest in South Wales, and are equipped with the latest machinery. They have the sole agency for South Wales & Monmouthshire for the new Cove Red Stone, which is a deep red sandstone; also Berry Hill Quarries, Forest of Dean.

In order to prevent their retreat from being followed up, the town bridge—then, like several succeeding ones, of wood—was set fire to by Leicester, he and his army falling, more or less leisurely, back into Herefordshire. "Henry (the Third), not unmindful of the loyal conduct of the inhabitants, and their vigorous opposition to the Earl of Leicester, built the tower of the Church as a testimony of his gratitude. His statue is placed in a niche in the Western front, but the head was struck off by the soldiers of Cromwell." This is the story told in Coxe's "Historical Tour through Monmouthshire." A more probable explanation as to the statue, is given by Mr. Freeman. This writer observes that the massive tower is said to have been built by Jasper Tudor, uncle of Henry VII. Jasper Tudor had a great fancy for building churches; and amongst others, he built the tower of Llandaff

Photo, A. & G. Taylor, Newport.

NEWPORT AND MON. HOSPITAL, CARDIFF ROAD.

Cathedral, which bears his name. The most prominent object on the west face of the tower, is the headless statue of a knight in armour; this is generally supposed to be the statue of Jasper Tudor, which was mutilated by Cromwell's soldiers, at the time of the Civil War.

In support of this version, we believe that the Tudor Rose can be discerned on the statue, which would certainly not have formed part of a decoration on an effigy of King Henry III., whether vain-gloriously raised by himself, or by any one else to his illustrious (!) memory.

Growth of Newport.

It is probable enough, quite apart from the erection of the great Castle by Robert, Earl of Gloucester, that Newport, situate as it is at a most convenient point on the right bank of the Usk, and only about four miles from where the river debouches into the Severn Sea, owed its rise in the first instance to this more advantageous position as compared with that enjoyed by Caerleon, being in fact about equi-distant between that place and the sea. As it progressed, the older and more famous Brito-Romano City, already greatly reduced, more and more decayed.

Photo, A. & G. Taylor, Newport.

CARDIFF ROAD ENTRANCE TO BELLE VUE PARK.

Photo, A. & G. Taylor, Newport.

PALMYRA PLACE, NEWPORT.

NEWPORT BRIDGE AND CASTLE. *Photo, A. & G. Taylor, Newport.*

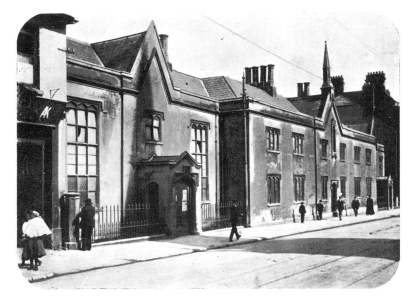

Photo, A. & G. Taylor, Newport.

THE OLD NATIONAL SCHOOLS (DISUSED) COMMERCIAL STREET.

Thus as time went on, to Newport accrued much of the consideration and importance which once had gathered around the famous City of Caerleon.

The Castle was naturally the dominating evidence of baronial power, the fortress into which, in the mind's eye, we may see mail-clad knights and men-at-arms, attendants perhaps on beauteous dames of high degree, entering "in all the pride and circumstance" of power. We may well imagine gaily bedecked galleys and barges making for the spacious water-gate. The New Town and Port itself were further protected by strong walls, with gates giving ingress and egress, so that the whole place must have been a stronghold of considerable strength, in days, too, when gunpowder and cannon were still unknown. Coxe, writing in 1799, describing the Castle, remarks, that "in the middle of the side towards the water, is a square tower, which seems to have been the keep or citadel flanked with small turrets, and containing the remains of a spacious apartment, called the stateroom, with a vaulted stone roof. Underneath is a sally port, leading to the river, with a beautiful Gothic arch, once defending a portcullis, the groove of which is still visible. At each extremity of this side are octagon towers, one of which, though much mutilated, is inhabited. To the left of the middle tower are the remains of the baronial hall, with a large fireplace; the windows are of the Gothic species, and richly decorated.

Photo, A. & G. Taylor, Newport.

LIEUT. GREY.

From an Oil Painting in the Museum.   By permission.

Evident vestiges of numerous apartments are seen in the area, and several chimnies appear in the side wall."

The Castle Gates.

The East Gate was by the Bridge, and the others, believed to be three in number, were at the opposite extremity of the town. Leland, the historian, writing in the 16th century, describes one as standing in the centre of the town, in fact as being in the High Street, " to passe through, and hard without the wall is the Paroche Churche "—(St. Woolos'). The "centre of the town" would be a very unusual position for a gate, unless intended as a portion of an inner defence, which it probably was. Unfortunately all trace of it has long ago disappeared. For all that, what was later known as the West Gate existed and was so used up to nearly the end of the 18th century. It is described as having been in the Gothic style and constructed of red grit sandstone, with a shield bearing the arms of Ralph Stafford, Lord of Newport. The West Gate was, as late as 1790, used as a town gaol. A small room in the centre over the arch of the gateway was applied to this rather ignoble purpose; a stone staircase leading thereto; but all have vanished.

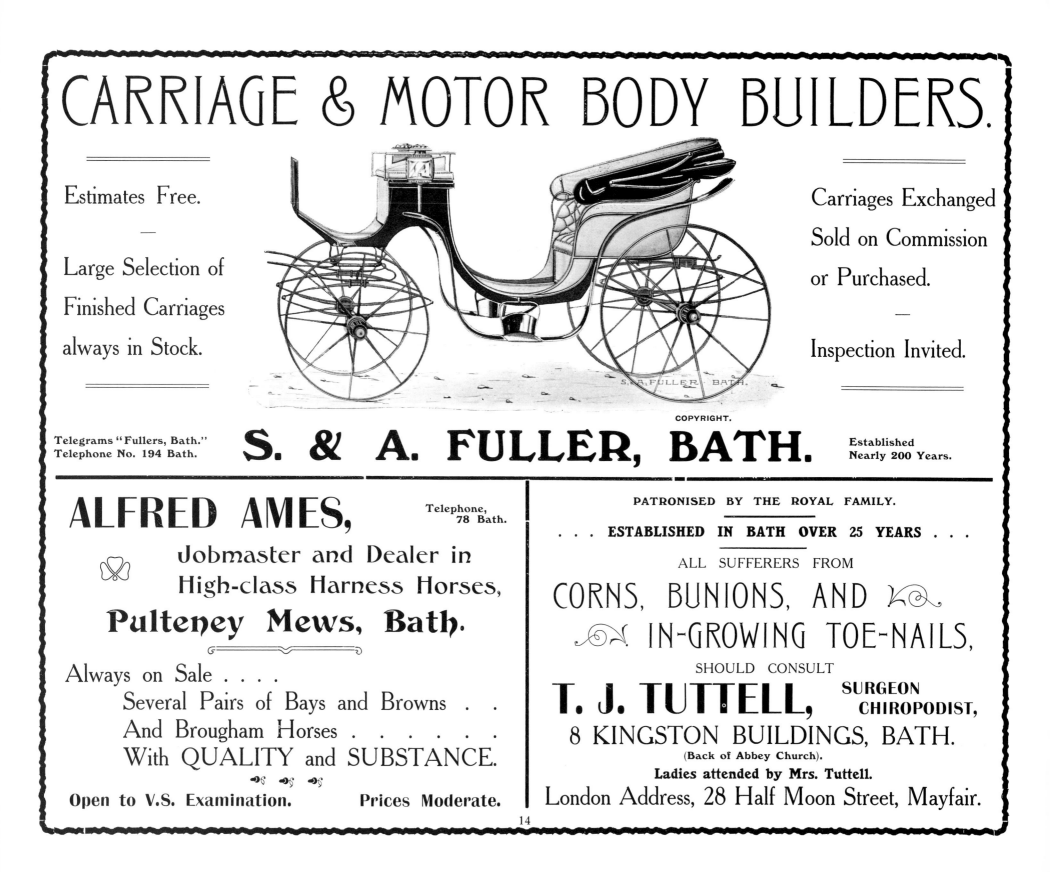
14

In 1799 (106 years ago), being in a ruinous state, it was pulled down. There were some inconsiderable iron remnants of the East Gate in position up to some years ago; these also have disappeared.

In fact, were it not for the ruined remains of the first Earl of Gloucester's noble Castle, nothing but little-consulted history and vague tradition would remain to tell or to indicate that Newport had a thriving and notable existence many centuries ere it finally settled down to the designation it now so well bears of NEW PORT.

Newport as a Fortress.

An interesting proof that Newport was at one time a walled town lies in its having in those days

Photo, A. & G. Taylor, Newport.

THE INTERMEDIATE SCHOOLS.

and for centuries an official known as the Murenger, whose duty it was to collect the murage, or the tax for meeting the expenses of repairing the walls of such fortified places. The house of Mr. Pennington, No. 53, High Street, has been identified as the Murenger's house. Probably this was the traditional site of that functionary's residence, for the office itself seems to have been abolished as far back as Edward the Second's time (whose inglorious reign extended from A.D. 1307 to 1327— Edward being murdered in the latter year in Berkeley Castle). The King issued a charter freeing the good men and true of the town from the imposition and burthen of it. The Murenger's House has been described as having been a large and imposing building, having a coat of arms on the richly ornamented front.

Photo, A. & G. Taylor, Newport.

THE RIVER, WITH STEAMER AT LANDING STAGE.

Photo, A. & G. Taylor, Newport.

MONMOUTHSHIRE COUNTY COUNCIL OFFICES, QUEEN'S HILL.

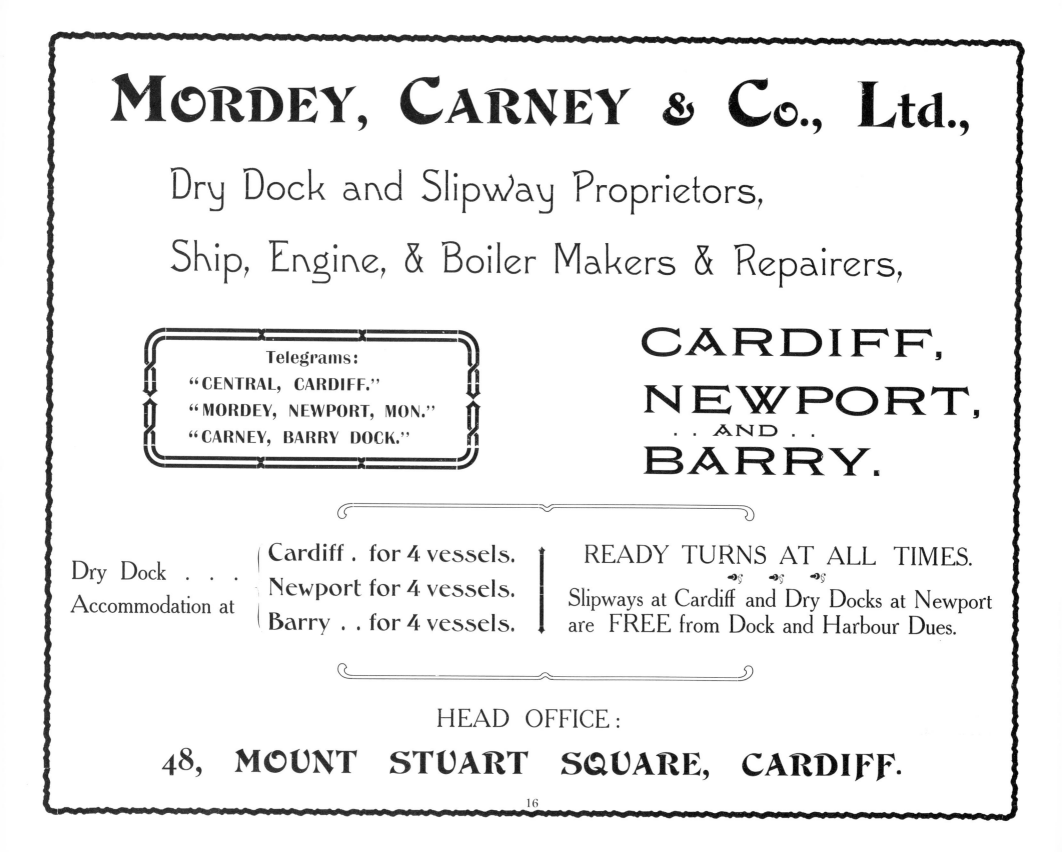

MORDEY, CARNEY & Co., Ltd.,

Dry Dock and Slipway Proprietors,

Ship, Engine, & Boiler Makers & Repairers,

Telegrams:
"CENTRAL, CARDIFF."
"MORDEY, NEWPORT, MON."
"CARNEY, BARRY DOCK."

CARDIFF, NEWPORT, .. AND .. BARRY.

Dry Dock . . . Accommodation at

Cardiff . for 4 vessels.
Newport for 4 vessels.
Barry . . for 4 vessels.

READY TURNS AT ALL TIMES.

Slipways at Cardiff and Dry Docks at Newport are FREE from Dock and Harbour Dues.

HEAD OFFICE:

48, MOUNT STUART SQUARE, CARDIFF.

16

THE NEWPORT PICTORIAL.

Early Charter Privileges.

From 1307 or a little later, to 1624, is of course a long stretch of over three hundred years. In the latter year King James the First bestowed a new Municipal Charter upon the town. Among other things, this gave the Corporation the important right to possess manors and lands to a value not above fifty pounds per annum (then a very large sum). In the interests of the townspeople it forbad what it styled "foreigners" and persons from other places outside Newport from selling goods in the borough, save at and during fairs; and it further fixed two general fairs for the town. Much of the glory of the old fair time has everywhere in England, under modern conditions, declined. The town has, however, still its fairs as follows:—On the 2nd Wednesday in April; Wednesday in Whit week; June 23rd for Wool; the 2nd Wednesday in August, and 1st Wednesday in November for Wool.

A Tale of Treachery.

An incident characteristic of the scenes of violence and lawlessness of the days when Newport Castle flourished in its greatness and grandeur is told, in which Henry II. comes out very badly. It appears

J. F. MULLOCK'S VIEW OF THE OLD DOCK, NEWPORT, MONMOUTHSHIRE, 1835.
By permission of the Library and Museum Committee.   *Photo, A. & G. Taylor, Newport.*

Photo, A. & G. Taylor, Newport.   DOCK STREET FROM NEWPORT BRIDGE.   17   BOARD OF GUARDIANS OFFICES, QUEEN'S HILL. *Photo, A. & G. Taylor, Newport.*

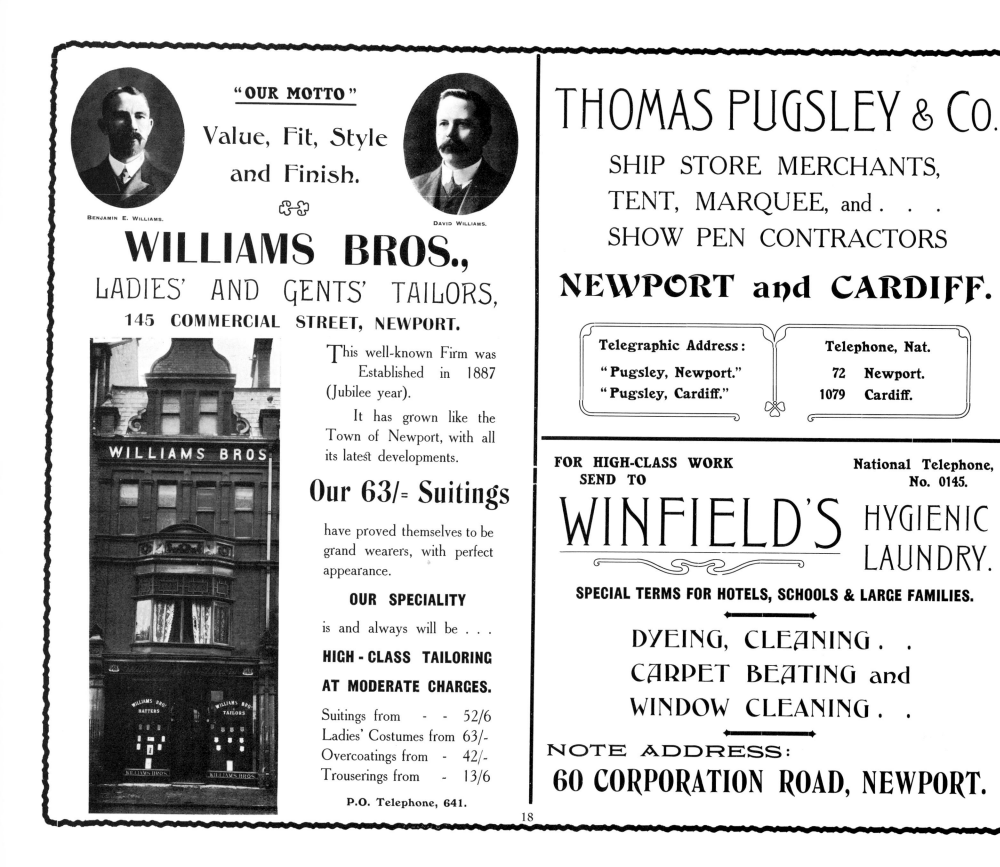
18

that Iorwerth ap Owen, a great Welsh Chieftain, who flourished in that King's reign, had suffered the loss of a portion of his domains, but, having recovered the greater part, Henry on his return from his visit to Ireland in 1172, found that Ap Owen had become once more quite a formidable Prince. The King therefore resorted to diplomacy and treachery to overcome him, professing a desire to arrange terms of amity and friendship. A conference between the King and the Prince was arranged to be held on neutral border grounds, and a safe conduct was granted by the King. Owen, the eldest son of the Welsh Prince and ruler, proceeded to his father's camp. On the way, a body of soldiers rode out of Newport Castle, and apparently acting under instructions, captured and assassinated the young Prince. Naturally Iorwerth, insensate at this brutal and dastardly crime, and burning with a desire for revenge, turned back into Wales and called on his countrymen to punish the wrong doers. Large bodies of the warlike Welsh, nothing loth, flew at once to arms. The English army was defeated, and the marches laid waste, threatening also both the cities of Gloucester and Hereford. Thus was an act of deep treachery and cruelty punished as such crimes deserved to be punished. But even in those days of violence and rapine, the innocent must necessarily have suffered with the guilty. (*Vide* Powell's History of Wales).

THE TRANSPORTER BRIDGE.   *Photo. A. & G. Taylor, Newport.*

Another Crime.

There is still another story, but less authenticated, of an act of treachery in connection with this great mediæval fortress. It was still a place of strength and importance in Stuart days, and it is said that when the Protector's forces were encamped on Fair Oak Hill, with the view of taking the Castle, a person well disguised, offered to the General for a substantial consideration, to betray the besieged by means of a secret underground passage leading into the Castle. The traitor's offer was accepted, the Castle taken, but no sooner was the desired success attained than the traitor wretch was himself hanged by those to whom he had

Photo, A. & G. Taylor, Newport.

ON THE CHEPSTOW ROAD.

Photo, A. & G. Taylor, Newport.

IN GIBBS ROAD, MAINDEE.

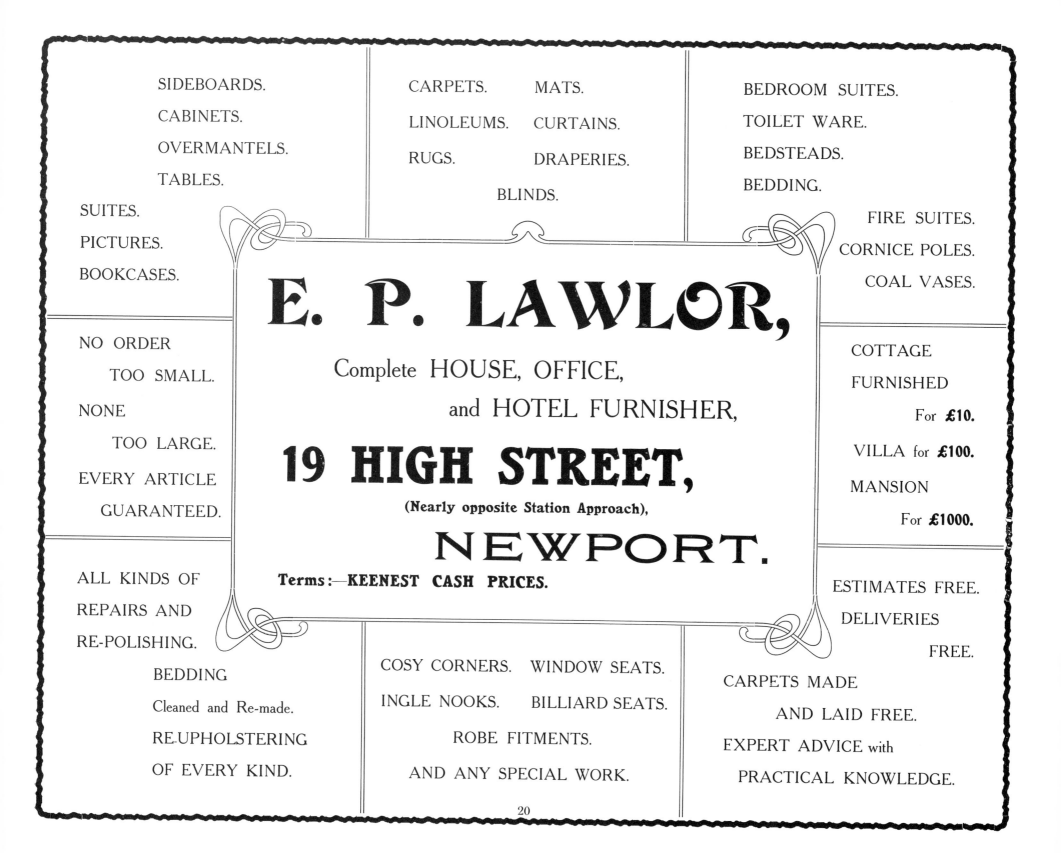

SIDEBOARDS.
CABINETS.
OVERMANTELS.
TABLES.

CARPETS. MATS.
LINOLEUMS. CURTAINS.
RUGS. DRAPERIES.
BLINDS.

BEDROOM SUITES.
TOILET WARE.
BEDSTEADS.
BEDDING.

SUITES.
PICTURES.
BOOKCASES.

FIRE SUITES.
CORNICE POLES.
COAL VASES.

E. P. LAWLOR,

Complete HOUSE, OFFICE,
and HOTEL FURNISHER,

19 HIGH STREET,

(Nearly opposite Station Approach),

NEWPORT.

Terms:—KEENEST CASH PRICES.

NO ORDER
TOO SMALL.
NONE
TOO LARGE.
EVERY ARTICLE
GUARANTEED.

COTTAGE
FURNISHED
For £10.
VILLA for £100.
MANSION
For £1000.

ALL KINDS OF
REPAIRS AND
RE-POLISHING.
BEDDING
Cleaned and Re-made.
RE-UPHOLSTERING
OF EVERY KIND.

COSY CORNERS. WINDOW SEATS.
INGLE NOOKS. BILLIARD SEATS.
ROBE FITMENTS.
AND ANY SPECIAL WORK.

ESTIMATES FREE.
DELIVERIES
FREE.
CARPETS MADE
AND LAID FREE.
EXPERT ADVICE with
PRACTICAL KNOWLEDGE.

20

so foully given victory. When the Monmouthshire Canal was being made, portions of this passage were said to have been discovered; unfortunately, however, the matter seems to have been allowed to rest there.

The Castle Proprietors.

The architectural style of the Castle shows it to have been of the late Perpendicular order, with round-headed arches.

Naturally the rough and turbulent times alluded to left their mark upon the once noble pile. It passed through many hands. At one time it was the property of the powerful Richard de Clare, Earl of Gloucester and Hereford; then it passed to the De Spencers, leaving them on the attainder of Edward, the third Duke of Buckingham; reverted to the Crown; was then granted to Hugh de Audley; passed into other hands; and, as above stated, was besieged and captured by Cromwell's troops. In more modern days it passed by marriage into the family of the late Earl of Powys; was sold to Charles Van, Esq., of Llanwern, who granted a lease of the tower next the bridge to the Rev. Mr. Burgh (the ownership of the Manor of Newport being in his family), his father having exchanged the remainder of the Castle with Wm. Kemeys, Esq., of Maindee. Finally, the above mentioned tower, and the parts between it and the

HIGH STREET. Photo, A. & G. Taylor, Newport.

Photo, A. & G. Taylor, Newport.

THE GROUNDS, NEWPORT AND MON. HOSPITAL.

Photo, A. & G. Taylor, Newport.

CLARENCE PLACE, SHOWING JUNCTION OF ROADS.

Castle, were purchased by the Marquis of Worcester (afterwards the Duke of Beaufort). The greater portion of the Castle is now in the possession of Lord Tredegar. It is, however, hoped that it will yet be secured on behalf of the town and be utilised for more satisfactory purposes than its designers ever probably imagined it would be, namely: as an Art or such-like Gallery.*

At all events, having fulfilled its purpose, after nearly eight hundred years small portions of it, roofless towers and partly useless walls, now alone stand to remind even the most heedless passer-by, of

Photo, A. & G. Taylor, Newport.　　COMMERCIAL ROAD FROM TOWN HALL.

Photo, A. & G. Taylor, Newport.

MURENGER HOUSE, 53 HIGH STREET.

how stately and strong was once Newport's Castle, and how bravely it protected the little town sheltered under its walls from foe by river and by land.

Old Newport.

That ancient town has also disappeared, but we have some authentic record of its appearance as set forth in verse in Churchyard's Work, at the close of the 16th century (1587), and entitled "The Worthines of Wales," as follows:

"A toune nere this;* that buylt is all a length,
Call'd Neawport now, there is full fayre to viewe:
Which seate doth stand for profite more than strength,
A right strong bridge is there of timber newe.
A river runnes, full nere the Castle wall;
Nere church likewise, a mount behold you shall,
Where sea and land to sighte so plaine appeeres,
That there men see a part of five fayre sheeres,†
As upward hye, aloft to mountain top
This market toune is buylt in healthful sort;
So downeward loe is many a merchant's shoppe,
And many sayle to Bristowe from that port.
Of aunciente tyme, a citie hath it bin;
And, in those daies, the Castle hard to win;
Which yet shewes fayre, and is repayrd a parte,
As things decayed, must needes be helpt by arte."
　　* Caerleon.　　　† Shires.

Photo, A. & G. Taylor, Newport.

PORTICO TOWN HALL.

* Since this was written, reports have appeared to the effect that negotiations were contemplated as between Lord Tredegar and the Corporation, in order to restore, and then use the building as a Museum. The tower next the bridge belongs to the Town, and the remainder to his lordship. Should Lord Tredegar become the sole proprietor of the Castle remains, it is pretty well assured that his lordship will see that the noble pile will be put to the best use.

MORRISH'S
COMMERCIAL **HOTEL,** **AND FAMILY**
NEWPORT, MON.

Telephones:
National - - 79
Post Office - 522

Telegrams and
Postal Address:
"Morrish's Hotel."

MORRISH'S COMMERCIAL HOTEL

THIS WELL-KNOWN HOTEL is the Largest and Oldest Established Unlicensed Hotel in Newport, and is situated within two minutes' walk of the General Post Office, Railway Station, Town Hall, Metal and Corn Exchange, Electric Tram Centre, &c. It comprises: Commercial, Coffee, and Private Sitting Rooms, Writing and Smoke Rooms, Billiard Room, Stock Rooms, and 35 well-appointed Bedrooms. Electric Light, and heated throughout with hot water radiators.

Highly Recommended for Comfort and Cleanliness.

Open for Night Express and Mail Trains.   Boots in Attendance.

C.T.C. QUARTERS.   **H. W. Morrish, Proprietor.**

24

THE NEWPORT PICTORIAL.

From the foregoing it is clear that over three hundred years ago Newport was a busy market town, with a brisk shipping connection with Bristol, and that the Castle was a fortress still to be reckoned with by any desirous of gaining the ascendancy in these parts.

In 1764, a plan then taken, showed that the town and liberties consisted of High Street and Church Street,—now known as Stow Hill; and some few straggling houses; there were 192 tenants, and the houses were of the gable type.

Thirty two years later, in his History of Monmouthshire, Williams gives the following description of Newport:

"The situation of the town is happily and conveniently chosen—on the banks of a large and navigable river; in a district extremely fertile; and where the mineral treasures of the hills may be conveyed by canals for exportation."

A year later (1797), in a description of it in a Tour, the same Author says:

"The bridges over the Uske, both at Newport and Caerleon, and over the Wye at Chepstow, are built upon exceeding high piles of wood; they are floored with boards, which are always loose, but prevented from slipping by small tenons at their ends: the precaution of having the boards unfixed is not unnecessary, as the tides in these rivers sometimes rise to a stupendous height, and would otherwise blow up the bridges."

Photo, A. & G. Taylor, Newport.

VIEW OF NEWPORT FROM ALBERT TERRACE, TOWARDS GOLD TOPS AND QUEEN'S HILL.

Newport Bridge.

The present fine stone bridge superseded the foregoing in 1800, costing a little over £10,000, having been erected by David Edwards. In 1866, from the plans of Mr. T. Dyne Steel, C.E., of Newport, the bridge was widened, and later the approach from High Street was levelled.

There are (or were some years ago) traces of the foundations of two previous bridges (timber structures) to be seen near the Bridge Hotel and Beaufort Wharf, and the earliest mention of a bridge occurs in a grant of Morgan, son of Morgan, to the Gloucester Convent, of lands near the bridge, which was made between 1072 and 1104.

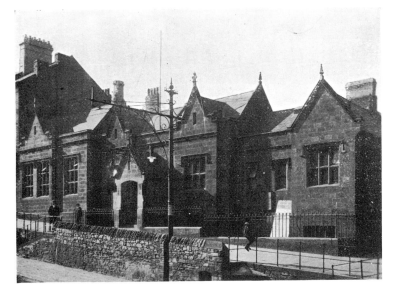

Photo, A. & G. Taylor, Newport.

CORPORATION BATHS, STOW HILL.

Photo, A. & G. Taylor, Newport.

GIBBS ROAD, MAINDEE.

Development of Modern Newport.

Early Newport.

Under its old Charters, Newport went dreamily on, more or less wisely governed by its Mayors, Aldermen and Councillors, for many generations. It was not until the last decade of the 18th century, a period in modern history which shook up many greater places than Newport, and overturned greater dynasties than have ever swayed the once warlike border town of Wales, that we hear much of it. Whether it was due to the upheaval of the French Revolution, and the general spirit of unrest which that prodigious event of world-wide significance brought about, or to causes of more local growth, need not be inquired into; but certain it is that, in 1792, an Act of Parliament was sought to be obtained to authorise the making of the canal from Newport to Pontypool, with a branch to Crumlin. After much financial and other difficulties had been overcome the Crumlin branch of the Canal was opened in 1798—a year which saw Napoleon Buonaparte smashing up all the old Powers of the Continent, and Ireland found herself in the throes of a great rebellion. The Pontypool branch was opened in 1800.

The Tredegar Iron Works were established at Bedwellty in 1800; two years later Parliamentary powers authorised the Company, Sir Charles Morgan and the Monmouthshire Canal Company, to make a line or tram road from the Sirhowy Furnaces to Newport, and this was opened in 1808.

Photo, A. & G. Taylor, Newport.

VIEW OF GRIDIRON AND MAINDEE FROM FRIARS STREET.

Photo, A. & G. Taylor, Newport.

CUSTOM HOUSE, DOCK STREET.

It may be said that the modern development of Newport first dated from this period, for the canals and tramroads affording good and cheap means of transport, led to the opening of Collieries and Iron Works, products which naturally gravitated to Newport for export, and as naturally led in time to the provision of suitable wharfage and dock accommodation.

At all events, we find that on the formation of the Tredegar Wharf Company, in 1807, it obtained from the then Sir Charles Morgan a lease (for 99 years) of about 200 acres of land, described as "adjoining the small town of Newport;" and working on the comparatively small capital of £16,000, laid out a street extending for a mile from the Westgate Inn of those days to Pillgwenlly. The Company formed wharves at that place for the use of the staple industries of the district.

Photo, A. & G. Taylor, Newport.

THE LOCKS, ALLT-YR-YN.

What the railways are to-day to Newport need hardly be dwelt upon. It is sufficient to say that no port in the country has in practice, though no doubt improvable in certain details—such as improved passenger booking offices and booking facilities,—better or more comprehensive arrangements for bringing to its capacious docks and wharves the staple products of the district, such as the rich coal and mineral deposits which lie at its door; just as the many and varied manufactures, of which Newport is now happily the centre, can be as easily dealt with at the same shipping and transport centres.

That thoroughfare is now known as Commercial Street and Commercial Road. Some other road improvements followed, one, perhaps the most important, being that which diverted the turnpike road to Cardiff from passing over Stow Hill and through Bassaleg, to pass along Commercial Street, and so by Tredegar Park to Castleton. This route was opened as the New Turnpike Road in 1812, and other similar great improvements rapidly followed. But the turnpike tolls on this and all other roads have long since been wisely abolished.

We thus find that the foundation-layers, nigh a century ago, of the then future prosperity of Newport, wisely combined the improvement of inter-communication, by canal, tram and roads, in order to promote it; and the later railways with their marvellous facilities had here, at all events, the public mind prepared for their advent and reception.

Photo, A. & G. Taylor, Newport.

TEMPERANCE HALL (INTERIOR).

Photo, A. & G. Taylor, Newport.

FIRE STATION, DOCK STREET.

BATH, THE FAMOUS ENGLISH HEALTH RESORT.

ROMAN BATH.

THE HISTORIC KINGS' BATH AND MINERAL SPRING.

GRAND PUMP ROOM FOUNTAIN.

Sufferers from Gout and Rheumatism should write for Illustrated Guide, post free on application to—
Secretary, Grand Pump Room, Bath.

CAERWENT.

Caerwent was in ancient times the chief seat of the Silures, but after the long Roman struggle with them, was finally captured on their overthrow by Julius Frontinus, A.D. 78. The Village stands on a Roman Street or the Julian Way. The Via Julia, leading from the mouth of the Severn to Caerwent, Caerleon and onwards to Neath, in Glamorgan, can still be traced. After the overthrow of the Silures, the Romans made Caerwent one of their principal Stations, under the name of Venta Silurum. The Village, up to some short time ago, retained considerable fragments of the fortress walls, 505 yards by 390, and in parts from 9 to 12 feet thick. From time to time, too, many Roman relics were found, including tesselated pavements, parts of columns and statues, and coins of Severus and Gordian III. Of late, active and persevering excavations have been in progress, in order to, if possible, bring to light many of the buried treasures of this once important and thriving Roman Station; for, like its once great neighbouring Roman city of Caerleon, the ravages of time and change have, with equal impartiality, swept over it, leaving little save the name and tradition of its former consequence.

We give Illustrations of several invaluable remains from Roman Caerwent, as carefully preserved in the Newport Museum; as also one from a photograph showing the same *in situ*.

By permission of the Museum and Library Committee.   Photo, A. & G. Taylor, Newport.

POTTERY FROM CAERWENT.

30

Newport's Later Progress.

For all these improvements and greater facilities for trade, the town's progress was not as rapid as might have been expected. Tolls on the road, and tolls on the town bridge did not help matters ; not to speak of salmon-netting, which as late as 1838, was carried on by boats above and below Newport Bridge, a pursuit of fishing quite out of line with anything like the present-day busy use of the river, by steamers and other large craft. From an æsthetic point of view, it may be regretted that the days of salmon-netting are not likely ever to return, any more than will the canal boats, perhaps, be seen disappearing from sight in the tunnel which, under the street, carried the canal and its towing path.

A Stormy Political Incident.

Unfortunately the political unrest, which under the name of Chartism, had, in the first half of the 19th century, arisen in the country, due partly to economic causes, and partly to the existence of grave political inequalities, and partly, no doubt, to the personal ambition of some restless spirits, had also reached to Monmouthshire. It was destined to bring about an alarming, though happily, as it proved, but a temporary state of trouble in Newport itself. Meetings in support of the so-called ' People's Charter," with its Five Points, were held in and adjoining the

Photo, A. & G. Taylor, Newport.

THE LYCEUM THEATRE.

Photo, A. & G. Taylor, Newport.

TREDEGAR HALL AND CONSTITUTIONAL CLUB.

town. These gatherings rapidly grew in numbers, and with them the disorderly and disaffected spirit hourly increased. Matters rather culminated on the 2nd of November, 1839, which happened to fall on a Saturday. The leaders in Monmouthshire were John Frost, a draper of the town, and at one time its Mayor and a magistrate; and Zephaniah Williams. These men, with their immediate friends and followers, formed the daring plan to take Newport, and, by blowing up the bridge, they hoped to prevent the Welsh Mail from proceeding to Birmingham. What was to be gained by this wild and seditious scheme, for the cause of "Reform," was not at all clear, but unfortunately for all concerned, an attempt was made to carry it out. Under the influence of the fiery appeals of the visionary leaders, men gathered from all parts, intending to march upon the town and port. These poor misguided folk being armed with anything they could gain possession of, so that with guns, swords, crowbars, pickaxes and so forth, they made up a motley, but for all that a dangerous as well as a large force in the cause of disorder and riot. It was estimated that these bands numbered from ten thousand to twenty thousand persons. They swarmed in from all the surrounding country, their appetite for rapine being whetted by the sacking of the villages through which they had to pass towards Newport, and

VIEW FROM THE OLD CEMETERY, CLIFTON ROAD.   Photo, A. & G. Taylor, Newport.

Photo, A. & G. Taylor, Newport.

CHARLES STREET.

Photo, A. & G. Taylor, Newport.

SOUTH-WEST VIEW OF NEWPORT FROM TOWN HALL.

CARDIFF ROAD, LOOKING TOWARDS THE GAER.

the male portion of the populations of which, they took the precaution of compelling to join their numbers. It was, however, not until Monday, November 4th, that they drew near the boundaries of Newport; a halt being made at Tredegar Park, while the Pontypool detachment (the leader of which was one William Jones) was coming up. Finally, this semi-military junction of forces having been effected, the motley "Chartist Army," in two strong divisions, marched upon and into the town, Stow Hill being the route taken by one, and the other entering through Charles Street, while both divisions met in the centre of Commercial Street. Fortunately for the town, and its safety, the Mayor and authorities, having been fore-warned, had made provision to meet the rioters with a military force, in the absence of which it is pretty certain that the lawless spirit abroad would have caused incalculable damage, and probable heavy loss of life as well.

It was about eight o'clock in the morning when the Chartist mob marched down upon the town, entering which and wheeling round, they rushed for the Westgate Inn or Hotel, where the Mayor was, and also a detachment (about a Company) of the 45th Regiment, under Lieut. Grey. The Mayor made a last appeal to the mob to disperse; but appeals and reading of the Riot Act

THE LOCKS, ALLT-YR-YN.

were equally ineffectual. The blood of the mob was up, and they had commenced firing upon the Inn. It was believed that the presence of the military was unknown to them: whether it was so or not, they attempted to force the door. The Mayor—Mr. (afterwards Sir T.) Phillips—and Lieut. Grey were in a bay windowed room, on the south side of the entrance, which accordingly commanded it. The Mayor, having opened the closed shutter, and authorised the military to use their firearms, Lieut. Grey gave the fatal word of command, when volley after volley was poured into the dense mass of infuriated men in front of the building. About twenty were killed, and many wounded; and then the disheartened Chartists, with their foolish leaders, beat a hasty retreat, leaving their dead and wounded in the open square. The Mayor did not escape injury, being shot in the arm as he was opening the shutter of the Inn window, to give the soldiers the opportunity of using their weapons. Probably his Worship's later conferred knighthood, was deemed to be some sort of consolation for the serious injury he had received in the discharge of his magisterial duty on this distressing occasion. Late in the same evening Frost was arrested, having lain concealed, after his defeat, in a small cottage in what is now the pretty residential suburb of Gold Tops. Williams and Jones were also apprehended, and all were tried, and convicted. The

Photo, A. & G. Taylor, Newport.

STOW HILL.

extreme and brutal sentence of being hanged, drawn, and quartered was passed upon them. This severe sentence, owing partly to a legal flaw that was discovered, and also, no doubt, from more merciful feelings prevailing, was subsequently commuted to transportation for life. Frost was after some time liberated; and died, peaceably and respected, at Bristol. Besides the honour conferred upon the Mayor, the Magistrates were in a letter thanked by the young Sovereign, the late Queen Victoria, for the loyal and vigorous conduct they had displayed upon this memorable but painful occasion. For a long time subsequently the Newport Chartists riots formed a theme in political discourses; but happily, under the improved constitutional laws, and Parliamentary and Municipal Franchises now long prevailing, the chance of the recurrence of any such outbreak, in this or any other part of the country, has disappeared, and, it may be hoped for ever.

An illustration of the attack on the Westgate Hotel by Frost and the other Chartist leaders and mob, taken from an old print, will serve to recall this alarming incident in the civil and political history of the good old Town.

Old Rural Newport.

It is, however, pleasant to be able to turn away from the records of this sad display of disaffection and disorder to brighter matters. Much of what is now busy or residential Newport was, at this time, green fields and most pleasant hillsides, the latter commanding, as happily they still mostly do, fine, indeed often magnificent views of hill, vale, river and distant sea. It would be useless to attempt to recall all the older features,

Photo, A. & G. Taylor, Newport.

VIEW FROM TOWN HALL LOOKING TOWARDS ALLT-YR-YN.

mostly obliterated not only from the eye, but from even the memory of the oldest inhabitants. One instance will suffice. Opposite the Church on Stow Hill was a square, on which was a small thatched Public House and stable, known as the Six Bells (and strangely enough), formerly the Vicarage, with the old tithe barn adjoining. About 1872, the picturesque old Inn and stable were pulled down, and the more modern Six Bells and Severn Terrace erected. But later, both the terrace and tithe barn were converted into the Children's Refuge. The Horse and Cattle and Pleasure Fairs, once held on Stow Hill, have also ceased to be held there, no doubt to the great advantage of that pleasant neighbourhood.

Upon the hill has been erected a new Workhouse, and thither were the inmates removed from the old Poorhouse, which stood and still stands (only now in a sorely neglected state) opposite St. Paul's Church, Commercial Street. Generously purchased by Sir Charles Morgan, this spacious building was converted into National Schools for the town.

VIEW FROM FIELDS ROAD.

Photo, A. & G. Taylor, Newport.

This was long before the era of Education Acts, whether of Mr. W. E. Forster or of Sir Wm. Anson; but it is strange that, with the memories of its elementary education days surrounding it, something tangible has not been done to rescue the old building from the miserable decay now only too obviously sweeping over it.

The Foundation of Modern Newport's Prosperity.

While the town was slowly developing with its improved roads and canal, the first great step in its real commercial development was taken by the opening of what is now known as the Old or Town Dock, in 1842. The building of the Town Hall had been started in 1838, but was not finished until 1842, being itself succeeded by the handsome pile which now extends from Commercial Street, and forms such an admirable architectural feature in New Dock Street.

With the construction of the Dock, its extension in 1858, the supercession of the tramways by the all pervading and irrepressible railways, with their steam power engines and convenient coaches, the making of the South Wales Railways and the completion of the New (Alexandra) Dock in the year 1875, a further impulse to the trade of the town was given. These finally launched the community on that stream of development and prosperity, which has no doubt been once or twice checked

Photo, A. & G. Taylor, Newport.

CORN EXCHANGE.

Photo, A. & G. Taylor, Newport.

DRILL HALL, DOCK STREET.

and dammed back in its flow, but only again to advance with still greater power, spreading on all sides increased comfort, prosperity, and municipal, social and personal comfort and happiness.

Looking at the antiquity of Newport as a fortified town and place of strength, and at the centuries which passed over it while it held that character, it is strange, (in face, too, of its natural advantages,) that it may be said to have only entered on its commercial development well within a century. It is true that iron was known to exist in the neighbourhood as far back as 1231; and in a charter so ancient as 1305 —six hundred years ago—the extraction of pit coal is referred to. It is curious, notwithstanding such facts, that even at so recent a

date as 1791, the number of vessels entering Newport was only 202, with a tonnage of 10,580. The entries outward were but little more, viz.: 247, and 12,349 respectively.

The population of the town, with its old charters and once magnificent Castle, was no more than that of a good sized village, to wit, 750. No doubt improvement soon followed the opening of the canal and Sirhowy Tramroad. The canal was a noble engineering work indeed, with its fall of 447 feet in 11 miles, — the great number of 14 locks actually being required to surmount the gradient within the short distance of one mile of Newport. Completed in 1798, as already stated; by 1801, the town had 221 houses and 1,135 inhabitants.

VIEW OF NEWPORT FROM TOWN HALL LOOKING TOWARDS CAERLEON. Photo, A. & G. Taylor, Newport.

Photo, A. & G. Taylor, Newport.
CORPORATION POWER STATION, CORPORATION ROAD.

Photo, A. & G. Taylor, Newport.
DOORWAY CASUAL WARD,
STOW HILL. THE PEMBROKE ARMS.

Photo, A. & G. Taylor, Newport.
THE OLD CEMETERY CHAPEL, CLIFTON ROAD.

The First Railway at Newport.

It is a most interesting historical fact that, so far back as 1802, an Act of Parliament was obtained, giving powers to construct a railway from Newport to Nine Mile Point—from which a tramway ran to the iron works at Sirhowy. Here was made one, at least, of Trevethick's large attempts at steam locomotion, long before Stephenson worked his steam engine at Stockton and Darlington. Trevethick, with Vivian, proved, in 1802, that a small steam engine could be constructed to draw a load of ten tons at a rate of five miles an hour, on parallel rails, a vast achievement at that time.

Photo, A. & G. Taylor, Newport.

DOCK MASTER'S RESIDENCE.

Newport's Development Last Century.

With the extension of railways to all parts, naturally, the development of Newport was rapid. Its houses had increased in two years (1839-1841) from 1,171 to 1,666, and in the latter year the population was 10,492. It nearly doubled in the next decade.

Note the following figures:—

1851, inhabited houses,			2,908 ;	population,		19,323
1861	,,	,,	3,666	,,		23,249
1871	,,	,,	3,970	,,		26,957
1881	,,	,,	5,447	,,		35,313
1891	,,	,,	8,588	,,		54,695
1901	,,	,,	11,845	,,		67,279
1906	,,	,,	12,778	,,		74,242 Estimated.

Photo, A. & G. Taylor, Newport.

EBBW BRIDGE, NEAR NEWPORT.

Thus, in 20 years, the population nearly doubled itself, and the number of inhabited houses increased over a hundred per cent. in the same period.

Its rateable value,—a very important test of the growth of a place on a financial basis—in 1881, was £153,730 ; in 1901, it was £354,276 ; considerably more than double ; in 1905, it had increased to £401,170.

Photo, A. & G. Taylor, Newport.

CLYTHA PARK ROAD.

The Port and Docks.

The Harbour (i.e. the River) of Newport is controlled by the Harbour Commissioners.

The Port itself starts from Rumney River, Rumney, and takes an imaginary straight line South East across the Bristol Channel, opposite St. Thomas Head, on the coast of Somerset, until it meets another imaginary straight line from the Flat and Steep Holmes, in the Bristol Channel, to Aust, Gloucestershire, there meeting Bristol Port boundary, and so continuing until opposite to Redwick Pill, Mon.; thence continuing across the Bristol Channel to Redwick Pill. It will be thus seen that the Port of Newport is pretty extensive.

In 1842 the first real effort to raise Newport's position as a Shipping centre, and to properly utilise its noble river, with a maximum breadth of some 1,000 to 1,200 feet, and with a tidal rise of about 38 feet (spring tides), and enormous river frontage, was taken—just over 63 years ago. This was the construction (above alluded to), at a cost of about £200,000, of what is now known as the Town Dock. It was opened on October 10th, of that year, with an area of only 4½ acres. With the considerable development that followed in the shipping (as well as in the trade of the town), it was decided to enlarge the Dock, which was completed and opened on March 1st, 1858.

NORTH DOCK.

The area of the old and enlarged Docks was in all 11½ acres. The whole constitutes the present Town Dock.

Trade followed the provision of traffic facilities. Just as out of the old Dock grew the new enlarged Docks so out of the new came the need for what was named the Alexandra Docks—divided into North and South. The first sod was cut on May 28th, 1868, by the then Lady Tredegar, the mother of the present Viscount Tredegar, the occasion becoming one of hearty general civic

ALEXANDRA (N. & S.W.) DOCKS & RAILWAY CO.'S STEAM MOTOR CAR.

congratulations and rejoicing. It was opened on April 13th, 1875, and the opening of this Dock caused the town to make still more rapid advances.

So that the Alexandra (Newport and South Wales) Docks and Railway Company (to give the Company its full title) possess three Docks, all entered from the river. They are the North Dock, South Dock, and Town Dock. The entrance from the river is only two miles below the Bristol Channel and open sea, and yet such are the inherited natural advantages of the position, in the protection afforded by the shelter of the river, that vessels may dock and undock at Newport without danger, even in the teeth of an ordinary gale.

A statement of the sizes and accommodation of the several Docks will be interesting and useful for reference and comparison :—

NEWPORT TOWN DOCK: Entrance lock, 220 feet long, 61 feet wide ; Dock, 1,753 feet long, 300 feet wide ; 11½ acres. It is about a mile nearer the town than the other Docks ; a fact which conduces to reduce charges on cartage, &c.; while the Dock has several other special advantages. Depth of Water, on outer cills, average spring tides, 31 feet ; ditto, average neap tides, 20 feet ; average depth in Dock 26½ feet. This Dock is practically in the heart of the town.

ALEXANDRA SOUTH DOCK: This Dock is nearest the mouth of the river, connected with the North Dock by a channel 65 feet wide, and spanned by a movable girder bridge ; trumpet-mouthed entrance, 340 feet wide ; entrance lock, 503½ feet long, 72 feet wide ; Dock, 1,500 feet long, 550 feet wide ; area, 20 acres. Depth of water, on outer cills, average spring tides, 35 feet ; ditto, average neap tides, 25 feet ; average depth in Dock, 30 feet. This and the North Dock are electrically lighted.

NORTH DOCK : Trumpet-mouthed entrance, 300 feet in width ; entrance lock, 350 feet long, 65 feet wide ; Dock, 2,500 feet long, 500 feet wide ; area, 28¾ acres. Depth of water, on outer cills, average spring tides, 35 feet ; ditto, average neap tides, 25 feet ; average depth in Dock, 30 feet.

Vessels of the largest size, it may be superfluous to say, can navigate the river without difficulty and can have access or exit day or night from these noble Docks, with the greatest ease. There are also all possible advantages to shippers and others in regard to the navigation, port, and wharfage Dues, &c., in order to facilitate and render profitable the use of the Docks and Harbourage.

The Company also own a Dry (Graving) Dock, 523 feet long by 74 feet wide, connected with the North Dock by an entrance 50 feet wide, with a depth of water on cill of 20 feet, and entered from the Alexandra Wet Dock.

There are in the Port, besides the above, six private Dry Docks, one being 708 feet long, with entrance 65 feet wide. These are entered from the river.

The Alexandra Docks & Railway Company have their own railway from the Merthyr, Rhondda, and Aberdare Valleys.

The net-work of sidings and main lines surrounding the Docks extend to over 50 miles, and additions are constantly being made.

Shiploading and Unloading Facilities.

We need not enlarge upon all the care, skill and expense lavished upon providing the Docks with the very latest and best appliances for the discharge and intake of cargoes. For instance, coal can be shipped at the Docks, and the work carried on night and day, by the use of nineteen hydraulic staiths, and by the use of movable hoists two hatches can be loaded at once.

The hydraulic tips for coal are so constructed that they are capable of bunkering any vessel afloat, be she ever so high out of the water.

Nothing appeals more strongly to the coal shipper and the shipowner than the words "quick despatch," and Newport has striven, and successfully striven, to beat records in this direction.

VIEW OF ALEXANDRA DOCKS.

At Newport Docks the highest vessel can be loaded or bunkered with the greatest facility.

Large quantities of coal—40,000 to 50,000 tons—can be stored in railway wagons on the sidings ready for immediate shipment. As there are three lines leading to each tip, in case of "mixing" there is no necessity for marshalling in a cramped space and under pressure of work.

The method of tipping tends still further to promote dispatch. The loaded wagon is run along a low level road on to the hydraulic hoist, then lifted, and tipped into the ship. The empty wagon, instead of again being lowered to the level it started from, is returned on a high level road. This system enables the work to be carried on in a steady and un-interrupted manner. The only limit, in practice, is the neces-sity of trimming cargoes in the hold, and the use of anti-breakage cranes and boxes in lowering the first portions.

The arrangements for screening, weighing (which is done along-side ship), reducing breakage and so on, are of the most com-plete character.

Shipping is carried on continuously by day and night, and there is no extra charge for night labour. Coal shipping is also carried on at hoists on two River Jetties (owned by the Company), adjoining the North Dock. These jetties are suitable for small vessels engaged in the coasting trade, up to 200 tons net register.

It has been seen that the Docks are in direct railway communication with the pits, and coal is often in process of being shipped within eight hours of its winning in the mines. It addition to the excellent services of the Great Western Railway Company, the Alexandra Company have their own line running through Caerphilly to Pontypridd, which brings them into direct touch with the Western side of the Coalfield.

Thus many thousand tons of coal can be shipped day by day, working 24 hours; there being accommodation for from 4,000 to 5,000 waggons. And as the coal is brought direct from the Collieries, the advantages gained in rapid and economic loading are enormous.

Quick dispatch formerly meant a week for 3,000 tons; but as the facilities have increased so the loading time has lessened until now the Alexandra Company can, and indeed have, put 11,000 tons of coal in a steamer in 36 hours. This is achieved by progression in equipment.

What is true of the export of coal, holds equally good of that of iron ore, pyrites, manganese, timber, and the almost innumerable other raw or manufactured or partly manufactured goods which Newport exports and imports to and from, practically, all parts of the globe.

Among the recent improvements and additions to the equip-ment of the Newport Docks may be noted the following:

A new Quay on the East side of the South Dock has lately been opened, and is probably the most im-portant of the many new progressive works recently undertaken by the Company. It is 800 feet in length and is splendidly equipped with hydraulic machin-ery for dealing rapidly with general export and import merchandise. A large warehouse 200 feet long by 70 feet wide, with provision for overhead travelling crane and gantry, is also provided. Eight hydraulic cranes have been erected along the quay, all of them of the most approved modern type. Extensive sidings have also been laid down, linking this new quay and warehouse with the Dock Railway system in direct communication with the Trunk Lines of the kingdom.

The power required for operating all the machinery of both the Alexandra and Town Docks is developed at the new Central Hydraulic

SOUTH DOCK.

Power Station, Alexandra North Dock (opened in November, 1904). This is equal to any similar installation in the country.

The Docks are completely equipped with electric light, the current being generated at the Company's Station on the Dock premises.

Electric pumping plant, with a capacity of 1,000,000 gallons per hour, has also been constructed for use in Dock pumping in emergencies of abnormal drought.

The increasing area of the Docks has necessitated additional plant for dredging purposes, and a new 750-ton bucket ladder-hopper dredger is now working in conjunction with a 400-ton steel hopper barge.

The Company possess two powerful tug-boats, the "Horace" and the "Wolfhound"; twin screw vessels equipped with fire-engine, salvage appliances, search light and electric light. The latter fine vessel has, by the way, a Board of Trade passenger certificate for 95 persons.

All these subsidiary improvements and additional appliances only tend to fill in a portion of the Scheme of Development, of which we shall have more to say further on, and are all focussed upon the guiding principle which is actuating all movements at the Newport Docks,—namely: Efficiency in handling Over-sea Commerce.

And as proof that the note of efficiency along the lines of commercial undertakings is surely echoed by increased prosperity, we cannot do better than quote the following.

Statistics of Progress.

It is not within the purview of this book to give, or to bewilder its readers with columns and pages of statistics, however valuable in hemselves. They may, however, be profitably studied in the

EAST QUAY, SOUTH DOCK, SHOWING HYDRAULIC CRANES.

important official reports. We may here remark that the comparative statement of the trade of Newport, therein given, shows that while the total exports and imports, or "General Volume of Trade," was in 1893, 4,221,151 tons; in 1904 it had increased to 6,330,627 tons. Taking the summary for the years 1903-4, we find that in 1904, the total imports were 1,263,243 tons, being a net increase of 98,074 tons over the total for 1903. The total exports were 5,067,384 tons, a net increase of 310,540 tons of exports for 1903. These figures give a total of 6,330,627 tons for 1904 (as above stated), against 5922013 tons for 1903, or a total increase of 408,614 tons.

Statement of Trade at Newport.

1903 and 1904.

IMPORTS.		YEAR 1904.	YEAR 1903.	INCREASE.	DECREASE	REMARKS.
Iron Ore	...	477,796	334,935	142,861	...	Foreign.
Iron Pyrites	...	11,585	4,634	6,951	...	,,
Manganese Ore	...	37,032	36,050	982	...	,,
Mang'nif'rous Ore	...	...	8,500	...	8,500	,,
Pitwood	...	251,022	250,280	742	...	,,
Phosphate	...	4,920	3,030	1,890	...	,,
Timber, Wood, &c.	...	79,652	70,602	9,050	...	,,
Iron, Steel, &c.	...	179,231	267,405	...	88,174	,,
Miscellaneous	...	20,071	19,307	764	...	,,
Iron, Steel, &c.	...	69,597	48,557	21,040	...	Coastwise.
Other Imports	...	132,237	121,869	10,468	...	,,
		1,263,243	1,165,169	98,074		Net Increase

EXPORTS.		YEAR 1904.	YEAR 1903.	INCREASE.	DECREASE.	REMARKS.
Coal, Coastwise	...	940,201	916,432	23,769	...	
,, Foreign	...	3,143,979	2,953,064	190,915	...	
Coke, Coastwise		431	116	315	...	
,, Foreign	...	18,371	15,166	3,205	...	
Patent Fuel, Foreign		51,266	36,054	15,212	...	
Iron, Coastwise	...	111,656	103,699	7,957	...	
,, Foreign	...	139,140	99,486	39,654	...	
Tinplates, Coastwise	...	19,941	25,004	...	5,063	
,, Foreign	...	14,772	11,188	3,584	...	
Miscellaneous	...	30,131	32,052	...	1,921	Coastwise & Foreign.
		4,469,888	4,192,261	277,627	...	
Bunker Coal	...	597,496	564,583	32,913	...	
		5,067,384	4,756,844	310,540	...	Net Increase

Contrast this flourishing state of things with what existed in 1843, just 61 years before. The number of vessels then entering the Dock was only 148; the registered tonnage, 38,712. The tons of coal shipped were 32,575; iron ditto, 12,033 tons; timber, imported, 2,455 loads; and the Dock earnings were the modest sum of £2,157.

In 1904 the ships, in the coasting trade alone, that entered, including their repeated voyages, were 6,594 (of which 3,884 were steam), carrying 1,607,855 tons; and the number cleared (British and Foreign), 6,177 (of which 3,466 were steam), carrying 832,187 tons.

In the same year, the number of vessels, sailing and steam, that entered and cleared with cargoes, and in ballast, from and to foreign countries and British possessions was, entered, 6594; cleared, 6177 total tonnage, entered and cleared, being 2,440,042 tons.

These figures indicate, even if there were no other evidences, that Newport's shipping trade, and commercial development, steadily progress along the line of regular increase and of consequent prosperity.

The Cheapest Port.

No doubt this enormous development is largely due to the fact publicly stated, and we believe not attempted to be controverted, not only that the general position and facilities of the Port, and Harbour, and Docks are unrivalled, but also that it is the Cheapest Port in the Bristol Channel.

Another important point in favour of Newport, is that it is the natural and best outlet of the great coal fields of Monmouthshire and Glamorganshire; while for imports, as well as exports, its railway accommodation through the Great Western, and London & North Western, and Midland systems of railways, combined with the systems of South Wales, give it the command of the whole interior of the country.

Midlands' Natural Port.

Newport is also, by reason of its geographical position, the natural port of shipment for the Midlands. It is only within the last few years that the splendid position of the Port and the facilities for handling all kinds of merchandise at the Docks have been generally recognised and made use of by the large manufacturing firms of the Midlands.

The statistics of general exports given show that the claim of the Port to rank as one of the chief export towns of the kingdom is amply justified, while confirmation is added by the facts that twenty-three lines of general cargo steamers run regularly from Newport Alexandra Docks to all parts of the world, and that some of the largest and most important works in the country are leaving the Midlands and taking up new quarters on the banks of the river Usk.

IRON ORE BERTHS, ALEXANDRA DOCKS.

The Alexandra (Newport & South Wales) Docks & Railways.

The Dock and Wharf Property of the Alexandra (Newport & South Wales) Dock Company, include :—Area of land for Quays, Warehouses, Yards, &c., 423 acres (approaching double the area of the old Borough of Newport, which, within the boundaries, was only 239 acres) ; Alexandra (North) Dock, 28¾ acres ; ditto (South) ditto, 20 acres ; Town Dock, 11½ acres ; Graving Dock, (575 feet long, on blocks), 1 acre ; Alexandra Timber Float, 10 acres ; and Blaina Wharf (on River), 2 acres. Total, 506¼ acres.

Developments and Extensions.

Some account has been given in the foregoing of the improvements recently effected—all part of the big scheme for development and extension formulated by a far seeing and alert Directorate, and carried into successful being under the direction of their General Manager, Mr. John Macaulay.

These new works, already in utilisation, are but a tithe of the improvements projected, and which are well in process of evolution. Every device of modern skill and progress is being pressed into service.

The work of Dock extension, already employing a small army of over 1,000 men, in the hands of Messrs. Easton Gibb and Son, the Contractors, briefly consists in the extension of the present South Dock in a westerly direction. Land to the extent of 40 acres is being taken in, including a bend of the river Ebbw (the latter fact raising an engineering problem, the satisfactory solution of which called for the utmost skill, inasmuch as it necessitates the diversion of the stream itself).

This addition of 40 acres will, when completed, increase the entire water area of the Newport Docks to the fine total of 101 acres.

Another important feature is the new river wharf, 400 feet in length, now in course of construction, built upon the ferro concrete system and equipped with hydraulic cranes and ample siding accommodation. In addition to the foregoing, two coaling jetties are in course of building, with improved appliances so arranged that vessels may be loaded alongside at any state of the tide, a facility hitherto impossible in the river at low water.

We understand that probably the most important project included in the developmental scheme is that which will be placed before Parliament in the coming 1906 Session, involving the construction of a new deep water entrance to the Docks from a point near the junction of the river Ebbw with the Usk. This will consist of an entrance channel to the extension (now in progress) of the South Dock, in a westerly direction from Pilots' Pill, and will permit of the admittance of vessels over a much greater range of tide than hitherto.

The present article, in dealing with the advantages of Newport as a port of shipment, has been confined to the simple statement of facts—a statement of an unique equipment for dealing with over-sea traffic—but it may be safely anticipated that whilst the Docks progress so surely will Newport progress also.

THE TOWN DOCK.

A Parliamentary Compliment to Newport.

The foregoing statements give force to the remark of the Chairman of the Committee of the House of Commons which, in 1889, reported in favour of the Bill, now The Newport Corporation Act, by which a large extension of area, particularly on the eastern bank of the river, was added to the Borough :—" We have here a rising Town, which is evidently making considerable progress, and which seeks expansion."

THE NEWPORT PICTORIAL.

Other Docks.

Besides the Docks of the above Company, there are the Graving Docks of Messrs. Mordey, Carney & Co., Ltd., known as the "Edith," the "Alice," and the "Mary" (the latter 350 feet long); and repairing berth in Jack's Pill, adjoining, 350 feet long. The "Mary" Dry Dock has a width of 60 feet, and draft 32 feet, and enables the firm to take in vessels of the largest size.

The whole of the Company's works are in a convenient and acccessible spot on the western bank of the Usk, distant from the Town Bridge about a mile.

Completeness and adaptability have made it one of the best known concerns in the Bristol Channel.

Then there is the Eastern Dry Dock, leased by Messrs. Lang and Williamson, and nearly opposite the entrance to the Alexandra Floating Dock. It is 357 feet long on the blocks, with provision to lengthen; width, 77 feet; and depth on cill, at ordinary tides, of 22 feet.

The Gridiron, belonging to the Harbour Commissioners, on the East Bank near the Bridge, is capable of taking a vessel 244 feet long.

The Great Western Wharf was constructed in 1875, on the East bank of the river, and is in direct communication with the Great Western main line of railway, and has great capacity for discharging and loading.

MASONIC HALL, DOCK STREET.   Photo, A. & G. Taylor, Newport.

COAL SHIPPING—NORTH DOCK.

44

Photo, A. & G. Taylor, Newport.
NEWPORT & COUNTY LIBERAL CLUB.

THE NEWPORT PICTORIAL.

"Quick Despatch" at the Docks.

There is quite a number of examples of the quick despatch in loading. A few will serve to quote :—

Length of Vessel 216 feet, total cargo 1,473 tons, loading time 6 hours 40 minutes. Length of Vessel 455 feet, cargo 11,671 tons, loading time 36 hours 45 minutes. The same Vessel, with 120 tons less cargo, but with double screened coal, loading time 70 hours 5 minutes. Length of Vessel 445 feet, cargo 9,598 tons, loading time 43 hours 5 minutes.

A cargo of 2,167 tons of manganese ore was discharged between noon of one day and 11 a.m. the following day.

Among the Vessels using Newport are those of the "City" and "Clan" lines. The class of Vessels range from 324 feet in length, with 1,987 net registered tonnage, to 454 feet in length, and 4,801 net registered tonnage, and 444 feet in length, with 5,349 registered tonnage.

ALDERMAN TOM JONES
Memorial Tablet in Town Hall, unveiled October, 1905.

Newport and District Manufactures.

The list of general goods manufactured in and about Newport is a long and diversified one; and as we have dealt so fully with its main industries—Coal and Iron—we may here give some of the principal of the former :

Agricultural Implements; Angle Iron, and Castings; Bars, Blooms and Billets (Steel), Black Sheets, and Steel Sheets; Bolts, Nuts and Spikes; Bricks, Lime and Stone; Bridges; Roofs, and Constructional Ironwork; Building and Ornamental Bricks; Carriages and other Vehicles; Cast Iron Columns; ditto Pipes; Clothing and Shirts; Chemicals; Doors and Window Frames; Engines; Furniture; Bottles; Timber Work, generally; Steel Sleepers; Patent Fuel; Tiles and Stoves; Saddlery and Harness; Steel Sheets, Tanks, Tin, Terne, and Black Plates; Tobacco, &c., &c.

But, after all, no mere list of Manufactures can give half so good an insight into the productions and capabilities of Newport, as a stroll through its busy High Street, Commercial Street, Dock Street, and other business streets; and an hour or two at its fine Docks, and in viewing its various Wharves. Here will the Visitor observe the outward and practical signs of that great inner Mercantile and Manufacturing development, which has already placed the Town so high on the list of ports (eighth on the Board of Trade Returns), and on that of the Manufacturing Centres of the Country.

MARKET BUILDINGS, DOCK STREET.
Photos by A. & G. Taylor, Newport.

BOER WAR MEMORIAL TABLET.
In Town Hall Staircase.

General View of Newport.

Newport being so largely favoured by nature in its situation—a considerable portion of the town, and several of its most popular suburbs are placed on the rising hills, which at once shelter and command it, while adding picturesqueness to its appearance. The Visitor who desires to obtain a bird's eye view of the town, from any one point, cannot do better than surmount either Fair Oak Hill, on Maindee side, or Stow Hill, on the town side.

If the weather be to any degree favourable, he will be deeply impressed with, not only the fine

BELLE VUE PARK AND FOUNTAIN.   Photos by A. & G. Taylor, Newport.

WATERFALL, BELLE VUE PARK.

and imposing effect produced by the River and its long line of Wharves and Docks, and by the Town, but also by the undulating and far spreading landscapes, embracing mountain, hill, dale, river and sea, which all spread out before his delighted eye in panoramic detail.

In the Town itself no less pleasure, though of a different type, is to be derived in noting the extremely fine architectural development to be seen on every side in the more central portions. It is true that Newport, in this aspect, being quite a modern Town, one misses the quaint, old-timber fronted houses, and other links with the past, such as are to be seen in many other old towns in the land—Bristol, Chester, York, and Salisbury, for example. From this point of view, it may be remarked that the ruins of the Castle have a value far beyond any material estimate that might be placed upon them.

So long as they remain, or can be preserved, so long will they serve to unite, in a way that must appeal to all thoughtful minds, the new with the old, the modern with the ancient Newport—the Newport of bustling commerce and of maritime enterprise, with the

Newport of feudal times, of restless and ambitious barons; of midnight foray or daring sally: of gallant attacks by brave and warlike Welsh, and their repulse by no less brave and warlike Normans; and later, by equally gallant English. Thus should it be the desire of all to see retained, and preserved intact, as far as may be, these deeply interesting old walls and towers. As they look now, they appear as if, ere many more years have passed, they would indeed crumble into dust; and should this untoward, if undesired, fate overtake them, Newport will have lost for ever, a distinction as unique as it should be precious to every citizen within its boundaries, as we have no doubt it is, as also to many thousands far beyond.

The noble proprietor would doubtless regret its disappearance, as much as the most enthusiastic of archæologists; and the Corporation of Newport, would be well employed in using its influence to protect this ancient and noble relic from senile decay.

If, excepting the Castle and St. Woolos' Church, specimens of antiquity in architecture, houses or other buildings, are missed, there is, on the other hand, a large amount of pleasure to be derived from observing and contemplating the modern evidences of the architect's skill and the builder's ability which are to be seen on every hand, not only in the business thoroughfares, but also in the residential parts of Newport. Commercial Street and Dock Street abound with fine elevations, and the manner in which effect has in many cases been secured, under great disadvantages of space and position, is very remarkable.

THE GORSEDD STONES, BELLE VUE PARK.

UPPER WALK AND CARRIAGE DRIVE, BELLE VUE PARK.

IN BELLE VUE PARK.

Photos by A. & G. Taylor, Newport.

It is not surprising, perhaps, that the local Banks should be, not only figuratively but literally, to the front in this way; but other buildings, as the chief hotels, and the principal mercantile emporia, are fully equal, and in some cases superior in style. Effect has been secured not only by the designs architecturally, but also in and by the materials used. In this respect, the frequent use and application of the better quality of Bath Stone, sometimes, too, in juxtaposition to the local red sandstone or

BELLE VUE LANE, FROM CARDIFF ROAD.

CHILDREN'S PLAYGROUND, BELLE VUE PARK.

other local stone, has had the happiest effects. Bath Stone has, indeed, been so judiciously used by the architects and builders of Modern

Newport, as to afford, second perhaps to the City of Bath itself, one of the finest exemplars in the provinces of the remarkable capabilities of

THE FRIARS, BELLE VUE LANE (BACK VIEW).

THE FRIARS, BELLE VUE LANE (FRONT VIEW).   Photos by A. & G. Taylor, Newport.

THE PEOPLE'S PARK, PARK SQUARE.

this beautiful, lasting, and yet economical stone. This, in itself, is a decided testimony to the excellent judgment of the local architects in their choice of building material which is famous, all over the land, for long centuries.

At this point, it may be worth while calling attention to the very remarkable contrast presented in the Newport of 200, and 100 years ago, and to-day.

In 1704, an old plan of the Town gives it as containing two streets only, Church Street (now styled Stow Hill), leading from the centre of the Town to St. Woollos' Church (no doubt the original approach to this ancient and remarkable edifice); and High Street.

SIR CHARLES MORGAN STATUE, PEOPLE'S PARK.

ST. JULIAN'S HOUSE. Photos by A. & G. Taylor, Newport.

A few detached erections are also shown in this, but as there were in all rather under 200 tenements, the Town was originally of only narrow dimensions. A plan, by Coxe, of the City as it was in 1800, still shows Church and High Streets; in places continuous lines of buildings in each being indicated, and there is also Corn Street transversely between Church Street and the river, and forming a junction with the former and High Street; while the Castle and Friars are indicated, and the Mill at short distance from the former.

In 1803, a Tourist, in his published description, spoke of the Town as " dirty and ill built," and as " nearly comprised in one long street winding down to the bank of the Usk."

The wand of the magician, Improvement, has passed over Newport since those benighted and far-off days, and could that candid tourist, one Mr. Barber, see it as it now is, he would tune his song to a different key, or rather utter a panegyric instead of censure.

OLD DOORWAY, ST. JULIAN'S

Williams, in his "History of Monmouthshire," took a much finer and larger view of Newport, seven years before Barber's ill-natured remarks were published, when he said, "The situation of the Town is happily and conveniently chosen, and on the banks of a large and navigable river, in a district extremely fertile, and where the mineral treasures of the hills may be conveyed by canals for exportation."

Seeing that these thoughts and words first saw the light one hundred and eight or nine years ago, it must be admitted that the County historian was a man far ahead of his contemporaries, one, indeed, in whose path have, at a far later date, trodden the men who laid the foundation, or, who helped to build the Newport of Victorian and Edwardian days.

BEECHWOOD HOUSE, BEECHWOOD PARK.

The Electric Light and Tramways.

The introduction of the Electric Light into Newport, in 1895, was in due course followed, in 1904, by the opening of the fine system of Electric Tramways, which belonging to the Corporation, and thus to the Town itself, has superseded the old and slow moving horse-drawn cars system; and by a recent extension into the Stow Hill district, has brought all parts of the Town within easy, quick, and cheap reach.

No brighter or more lively picture is to be witnessed than the arrival and departure of the cars from the central point of the traffic—in Commercial Street and High Street—where forcible and striking illustration is afforded to the spectator of the immense development, on safe and prosperous lines, of the Commercial Capital of Monmouthshire.

THE STEPS, BEECHWOOD PARK.

BEECHWOOD PARK.

Photos by A. & G. Taylor, Newport   50

Crossing the River—
The Transporter Bridge.

A most important work is now in progress, and approaching completion. This is a Transporter Bridge, intended to improve cross-river traffic and thus to supplement, and of course relieve the existing Town Bridge, which, even with the bracketted widening of the footpaths, is no longer equal to the great and increasing public requirements.

This ingenious design is one of the most

THE DINGLE, BEECHWOOD PARK.

Photos by A. & G. Taylor, Newport.

THE GROVE, BEECHWOOD PARK.

remarkable and interesting of the later public improvements of the Town.

A full and technical description, without the aid of sections and plans, is more likely to puzzle than to enlighten the reader, who is consequently referred to the general illustration of the Bridge.

It may, however, be here briefly described as an overhead Bridge, by means of which, not only will the great rise and fall of the tides be provided against, but the navigation kept clear in all other ways. There are two steel towers of lattice work, 245 feet in height, one on each bank, the width between the centres of the piers being 645 feet. At a

height of 177 feet above high water mark (ordinary spring tides), a high platform, or girder, is suspended, supported by 16 high steel wire cables, passing over the top of the towers, and carried backwards for a distance of 150 yards to "anchorages" of solid masonry of about 2,000 tons each. To these the ends of the cables are fastened, and the platform so held firm in its permanent position. Across this run four lines of heavy rails, on which a low truck or frame runs, carried on four rows of fifteen wheels, one row working on the inside and the other on the outside of each of the two girders forming the platform. From this trolley thirty strong steel wire ropes or cables will be suspended within a few feet of high water mark, their lower extremities being attached to the car, in which every sort of traffic will be conveyed across the river. The car is 40 feet long by 30 feet wide, divided into three sections, the two outer for pedestrians (with room for

IN NEWPORT CEMETERY.

about 100 passengers), and the centre one for vehicles, taking six of the ordinary size.

Wire ropes worked by electric motors are used to draw the movable truck, on the upper platform, to and fro, along the railway; the motors being fixed on the river banks, and controlled by an attendant by means of an apparatus on the moving platform. Only a minute of time will be spent in the crossing.

The joint engineers are M. Arnodin, of Chateauneuf-sur-Loire, France, and Mr. R. H. Haynes, Borough Engineer. On November 8th, 1902, the then Mayor (the late Alderman Davis), laid the foundation of the western cable "anchorage." The site of the Bridge is from near the end of Alexandra Road, to where the approach road will lead into Corporation Road. The Contractor is Mr. A. Thorne, Westminster.

Newport Public Buildings.

The Public Buildings of Newport—that is edifices erected by and for the public, as distinguished from quasi-public buildings, such as banks, hotels, and insurance offices — are numerous. Several are distinguished, apart from their important uses, by high architectural skill and taste.

While the Municipal Corporations Reform Act of 1835, gave a great impetus to true local government throughout the country, it was in the case of Newport, more largely due to the spirit of enterprise evolved in the town itself, and the prompt action taken by its leading inhabitants that, aided by several local Acts, the boundaries of the Borough were on several occasions extended, and the Municipal territory and influence thus placed upon an unassailable basis.

Photos by A. & G. Taylor, Newport.
THE EXPLORATIONS AT CAERWENT, SHOWING PAVEMENT MOSAICS BEFORE REMOVAL TO THE MUSEUM.

To some extent the history of the development of the Town Hall is, in miniature, that of Newport itself. The old Municipal Building, dating from 1842, had within a little over thirty years been quite out-grown.

Very wisely, suggestions to remove the Town Hall from its central site were put aside, and means were found to gain the necessary additional space in Dock Street. So while the Town Hall proper dominates the High Street, the extension into Dock Street has given what may be considered a secondary frontage, both graceful and imposing. The Town Hall is in the Italian style, and is from designs by Mr. T. M. Lockwood,

PAVEMENT MOSAIC FROM CAERWENT.
By permission of the Library and Museum Committee.

PAVEMENT MOSAIC FROM CAERWENT
By permission of the Free Library and Museum Committee.

NEWPORT CEMETERY, SHOWING THE TWO CHAPELS.

of Chester, and Mr. E. A. Lansdowne, of Newport; and was erected by Mr. John Linton. It was opened in 1885, by the Mayor (Col. Lyne), advantage being taken of the visit of the Cambrian Archæological Association to the Town to carry out the ceremony on August 24th. The building comprehends the offices of a number of Departments which would otherwise have required separate housing.

There are also the Maindee Municipal Buildings, the Custom House, Harbour Commissioners, and Board of Trade Offices, General Post Office (now demolished to be superseded by a building more in keeping with present needs), the Corn Exchange, Coal and Metal Exchange, Provision Market, Corporation Baths, Free Library, Reading Room, Barracks, Museum and Art Gallery, Fire Brigade Stations, Baths, and Electric Power Works, County Council Offices, &c.

Buildings of a quasi-public character include the hotels, of which several such as the Westgate, King's Head, and Talbot are a great ornament to the Town; the fine Lyceum (formerly Victoria) Theatre; Empire Palace of Varieties; Albert Hall, Banks, Phillips Memorial Hall, Constitutional and Liberal Clubs, Tredegar Hall, Newport and County Hospital, Almshouses, Schools, and Churches and Chapels, &c.

The whole forms a list of which any city, however large, might be proud, and when it is remembered that all this remarkable development is mainly the work of the last forty or fifty years, admiration will be evoked for the public spirit, the farsightedness and the liberality which have attained such results, not only in so short a time, but often against great difficulties. It is only right to say that as a landowner the most closely identified with the Town, Lord Tredegar, has uniformly extended the most liberal, considerate, and warm support in helping forward Municipal development, without which, it would either have been next to impossible or greatly retarded and limited in its scope. What such support meant, only those on whom the responsibility of one act of progress after another really know and could fully appreciate. The Town at large, however, reaps the beneficent fruits to-day.

CLYTHA PARK.   Photos by A. & G. Taylor, Newport.

STOW PARK CIRCUS.

LLANTARNAM ABBEY.

CHARTIST RIOT, 1839—ATTACK ON WESTGATE HOTEL.

Ancient Ecclesiastical Edifices.

There is no doubt that, at one time, Newport possessed a Monastery or Friary; but after the Dissolution of Monasteries by Henry VIII., it probably rapidly disappeared through neglect and decay. Leland writing concerning the part of the Town, now known as Dock Street, near the Temperance Hall, speaks of the "House of Religion by the Key beneath the Bridge." This was a House of Augustinian or Austin Friars, the fraternity known in the Middle Ages as the followers of St. Augustine (the African Bishop).

The "Friars" (on Stow Hill) is stated to have been a house for White Friars, of the Carmelite Order; but the evidences of this must have

MUSEUM AND FREE LIBRARY. Photos by A. & G. Taylor, Newport.

largely if not entirely disappeared when it was rebuilt by the late Mr. Octavius Morgan, for a private residence, in handsome style (described as Gothic). The Bath Stone elevation, with the delicate warm or orange tint which that stone puts on with time, is very fine.

As to the order of Monks which occupied the building near the river one authority states that it was that of the Friars preachers of the Dominican, or Black Friars, at one time a very numerous and wealthy order in this and other countries.

Loose tradition, and a name attached to a locality or two, is all that now remains to indicate the presence and *habitat* in Newport of the Monastic Order and edifices of four or five centuries ago.

Apart from the Castle ruins, the architectural glory of Newport either from an antiquarian or ecclesiastical standpoint, is the ancient, singular, and deeply interesting Church dedicated to St. Woollos, on Stow Hill,—the acclivity from which some matchless views of Newport, and the river and district, may be obtained.

The Church is believed to have been founded in the sixth century, by the pious Welshman, St. Gwynllyw, and dedicated to St. Woolos (Latin, Gunleus). This latter name, (remarks Mr. Morris in his

NORMAN ARCHWAY, ST. WOOLLOS.

white ox with a black spot on its forehead, and when found it should be his country. Finding the mount, as predicted, he thereon built a church, and "on this spot continued to live, practising great austerities."

The historian Freeman, a high authority, considers it to be one of the most singular Churches in England.

Attached to the Church is a large western lady - chapel. This chapel of St. Mary, probably contains some part of the original structure. The entire building has been generally considered and described, by competent critics, as a fine specimen of grand, though unadorned, Romanesque architecture. This striking characteristic largely arises from the style of the doorway connecting the Western Chapel with the Nave, described by Freeman as the most remarkable architectural example in the whole country. A splendid specimen of Romanesque, it is thus not only unusual but also of great size, and especially so in its width, the arch being but little recessed for its dimensions, having only two orders, the inner one, however, being so wide that it occupies nearly the space of two. The usual Norman ornaments, billet and chevron are

ST. WOOLLOS, STOW HILL.   Photos by A. & G. Taylor, Newport.

TOWER, ST. WOOLLOS.

" Handbook of Monmouthshire "), by various colloquial changes in the 16th and 17th centuries, became corrupted into Woollos or Woolos. All accounts, he adds, agree that Gwynllyw lived at the end of the 6th century. On this point, the "Lives of the Fathers" (quoted in Coxe), says: "He (Gunleus) departed to Our Lord toward the end of the 5th century, and was glorified by miracles." The later date however seems the most probable on several grounds, not necessary to go into here. In his young days Gwynllyw bore the title of "Filwr"—the warrior. His father was Glewys, King of Glewysig. An old record states that a vision bade him seek for a mount whereon he should find a

Ebenezer Welsh Calvinistic Methodist (Presbyterian) Church, Commercial Street.

used; no decorative support pertains to the outer order, while in lieu of the ordinary slender nook-shafts of that style, the inner rests upon a pair of detached columns of considerable size, which thus forms the great singularity of the doorway. While having the composite order, the capitals are rather less classical than many other English examples.

The fact that the column is altogether different from the ordinary Norman style, and belongs to a type less widely departed from classical models, is indicated by its general appearance, size and position, the

St. Julian's Wesleyan Church, Caerleon Road.

Mill Street Congregational Church.

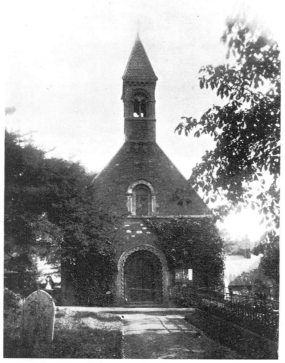

Malpas Church.

Havelock Street Presbyterian.

Photos by A. & G. Taylor, Newport.

DOCK STREET CONGREGATIONAL CHURCH.

TABERNACLE, COMMERCIAL STREET.

COMMERCIAL STREET BAPTIST.

COMMERCIAL ROAD BAPTIST CHURCH.

pedestal upon which it rests, the turn given to the neck moulding and by the conspicuous diminution of the shaft.

It is believed, and possibly with correctness, that the remains of the grand classic Roman architecture at the adjoining town of Caerleon, described as existing even so late as the 12th century, by Giraldus Cambrensis, in such glowing language, must have deeply influenced the minds of the architect or architects of this beautiful structure.

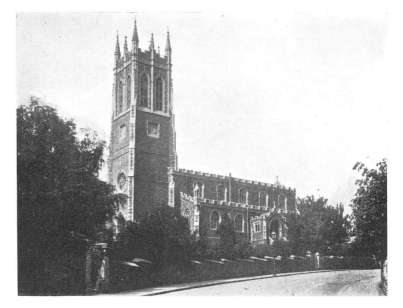

ST. MARK'S, GOLD TOPS.   Photo, A. & G. Taylor, Newport.

ST. PAUL'S CHURCH, COMMERCIAL STREET.

Upon this point, however, there may be differences of opinion, and there is certainly ground for wide speculation.

The Church also strikes one by its considerable length; as does Llandaff Cathedral, and Dorchester Church, though of course different; while what at the west end is discovered to be a large and lofty tower, looked at from the eastern aspect, seems insignificant, and might be deemed to be even a detached campanile. This effect is of course produced partly by the great length of the nave, but mainly by the interposition of the large western

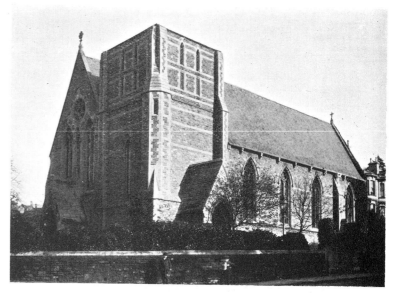

ST. JOHN'S CHURCH, MAINDEE.

ST. LUKE'S, BRIDGE STREET.

HOLY TRINITY, POTTER STREET.

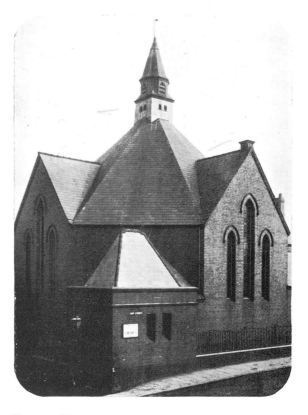

UNITED METHODIST FREE CHURCH, HILL STREET.

Photos by A. & G. Taylor, Newport.

MOUNT ZION (WELSH) CONGREGATIONAL.

ST. MARY'S (R.C.) STOW HILL.

ALL SAINTS, BRYNGLAS ROAD.

ST. JOHN'S, RISCA ROAD.

Photos by A. & G. Taylor, Newport.

chapel between it and the tower. No building better exemplifies the capabilities of what is deemed to be the wonderful Romanesque style,—which now admits the most lavish gorgeousness of decoration, and now stands in the serenest simplicity; while in neither case is its unrivalled solemnity and grandeur detracted from.

To this Church there used to be an end "Vesper Gallery," used of

ST. STEPHEN'S, ALEXANDRA ROAD.

VICTORIA ROAD CONGREGATIONAL.

course at the evening services. At the other end, is a stained glass window below which stands the altar. The gallery appears to have been at one time of stone; but wood has taken its place.

The Church consists of a chancel, nave, aisles, south porch, and a fine massive square tower. This is stated to have been built by Jasper Tudor—St. Mary's Chapel separating it from the Church.

Jasper Tudor, Earl of Pembroke, was the protector of Henry Tudor his nephew (afterwards Henry the VII.), from the

THE JEWS' SYNAGOGUE.

death of his father Edmund, 1456, till Jasper was, in 1461, obliged to fly from the vengeance of Edward the IV.; his nephew, the future King, being then consigned to the care of Sir Wm. Herbert, who protected him at Raglan Castle. Thence, after the battle of Tewkesbury, his uncle Jasper, returning secretly from France, carried him off to his own Castle of Pembroke, later embarking with him for France, but

ST. MATTHEW'S, HEREFORD STREET.

Photos by A. & G. Taylor, Newport.

both were detained in Bretagne by the Duke of that duchy, till after the accession of Richard III., whose overthrow afterwards, at Bosworth, left the way open for Henry to ascend the throne of England (1485).

The statue which adorned the west front of this square tower, described as one of Jasper Tudor himself, has suffered from mutilation, ascribed, like many other such pieces of vandalism, to Cromwell's soldiers. A statement that the statue in question was one of Henry III., given to the Church for the tower, in recognition of

BASSALEG CHURCH, NEAR NEWPORT.

CHARLES STREET BAPTIST.

The origin of the fine carved Reredos is thus told in an inscription on a brass plate:

"This Reredos was erected in Memory of HENRY JOHN DAVIS, Who for 31 years was Churchwarden of this Parish; And who died on the 5th April, 1903."

Photos, A. & G. Taylor, Newport.

WESLEY, STOW HILL.

the great services of the Earl of Gloucester in the war with Earl de Montfort, will hardly bear examination for one reason, that the tower belongs to a much later period,—probably early 15th century.

Apart from the architecture of this noble and unique Church, attention will be directed to the sepulchral monuments or remains of the same which it contains. The carved stone sepulchre of one of the Pembroke family has an arched canopy supported by fluted Ionic pillars. Within and beneath this is the effigy of a Knight in armour, his head reposing on a helmet, the whole style being that of the 15th century. The tomb has been much damaged, and the figures injured. There is under the archway the figure of a lady holding a rosary with cross pendant, executed in alabaster. A hatchment on one side of a fragment of broken panel, is believed to belong to the Morgan (Tredegar) family.

LLANTHEWY ROAD BAPTIST.

A small brass plate on the end of the Holy Table has the following:

"This Altar Table was Presented in Memory of the Mission, January 31 to February 10, 1904."

A brass plate to the memory of John Morgan, Esq., formerly hung on the altar, or Holy Communion rails. He died in 1702. It bore the following epitaph, and warning:

"He lived to dye, doe you so, I advise you, That death may never frighten or surprise you."

THE SCHOOL HOUSE, CAERLEON.

Photos by A. & G. Taylor, Newport.

HIGH STREET, CAERLEON.

To a more celebrated member of the family, the learned archæologist, Mr. Charles Octavius Morgan, M.P., brother of the first Lord Tredegar (born, 1803—died at the Friars, 1888), a tablet has been erected. The other tablets are numerous. The register of baptisms and interments dates from 1702, and of marriages from 1754.

Visitors will also note the lately added fine stained glass memorial windows, one being to the memory of Mrs. Whitehouse (died 1890). In the south aisle is a brass to the memory of her husband, Mr. Daniel Whitehouse, of the Gaer. The admirable oak pulpit was the gift of the late Mr. E. J. Grice, formerly Mayor of Newport, and the brass eagle lectern of Mrs. Cartwright.

In the south wall of the chancel is a memorial brass on an alabaster slab to the late Canon Hawkins, placed in position in 1897.

No apology is needed for thus dwelling upon this noble parish church of Newport, truly the mother church, founded by the piety and liberality of the early Christians of Newport and Monmouthshire, and extant to-day in almost its pristine beauty and full spiritual usefulness; whilst the adjoining Castle, the monument of military power and feudal grandeur, of temporal pride and ambition, is and has long been but a heap of fast crumbling ruins.

The other Church of England places of worship in Newport are St. Luke's Church (chapel of ease to St. Woolos), Bridge Street, erected in 1857.

St. Paul's, Commercial Street, erected 1840.
Holy Trinity, Potter Street.
St. Stephen's (chapel of ease to Holy Trinity), Alexandra Road, erected 1884.
St. Mark's, Gold Tops, erected 1874.
St. John the Evangelist, Maindee.
St. Matthew's, Church Road, Barnard Town, built 1892.
St. Andrew's, Lliswerry.
St. Julian's, Durham Road.
St. Mary's, Corporation Road.
All Saints, Brynglas Road, erected 1898.
St. John Baptist, Risca Road.
Union Chapel, Stow Hill.
St. Peter's (for Seamen), Temple Street, erected 1887.

Other Churches.

METHODIST.—Wesley Chapel, Stow Hill, opened 1884.
Commercial Road, re-opened 1899.
Mission Chapel, Price Street, opened 1885.
Victoria Chapel, Maindee.
Shaftesbury Street Chapel.
St. Julian's Avenue Church, opened 1902.

CONGREGATIONAL.—Mill Street (1640). The second oldest Nonconformist Church in the Principality.

    Tabernacle, Commercial Street, erected 1822, re-built 1894.

    Dock Street.

    Victoria Road.

    Mount Zion (Welsh).

    London Street, Maindee.

BAPTIST.—Commercial Street.

    Stow Hill.

    Commercial Road.

    Charles Street.

    Baptist Temple (Welsh), Commercial Road.

    St. Mary Street.

    Summer Hill, Maindee.

    Branch Chapel, Corporation Road.

    Alexandra Road.

    Llanthewy Road.

    Alma Street Baptist Church.

    East Usk Road.

PRESBYTERIAN CHURCH OF WALES.—Ebenezer (Welsh), Commercial Road (1829), re-built 1903.

    Havelock Street.

    Caerleon Road.

    Central Hall (Forward Movement).

    Malpas Hall   ,,   ,,

    Marshes Hall   ,,   ,,

    Corporation Road Hall   ,,

    Chepstow Road (now building).

UNITED METHODIST FREE CHURCH.—Hill Street and Portland Street.

PRIMITIVE METHODIST.—Station Street.

BIBLE CHRISTIAN.—Commercial Road.

    Christians' Meeting Room, Mountjoy Street.

    Christians' Meeting Room, Duckpool Road.

BRETHREN.—Room, North Street.

FRIENDS.—Meeting House, Charles Street.

YOUNG MEN'S AND YOUNG WOMEN'S CHRISTIAN ASSOCIATIONS.— Nos. 112 and 111 Commercial Street, respectively.

SOUTH WALES SAILORS' GOSPEL MISSION.—Wolseley Street Room.

CHRISTADELPHIANS.—Albert Hall Chambers.

SALVATION ARMY.—71st Corps, Cross Street Hall.

ROMAN CATHOLIC.—St. Marie's, Stow Hill.

    St. Michael's, Clarence Street, Pillgwenlly.

NORWEGIAN.—Church, Dockhead.

JEWISH.—Synagogue, Francis Street.

The Church of England has thus 15 places of worship (not including mission rooms).

Wesleyan	6	S. W. Sailors' Gospel Mission		1
Congregational	6	Christadelphians ...		1
Baptist	12	Friends		1
Presbyterian, or Calvin. Meth.	8	Salvation Army ...		1
U. M. Free Churches	2	Foreign		1
Primitive Methodist	1	Roman Catholic ...		2
Bible Christians ...	3	Jewish		1
Brethren	3			—
Christian Associations	2	Grand total ...		66

THE VILLAGE, CAERLEON.

MUSEUM AND CHURCH, CAERLEON.   Photos by A. & G. Taylor, Newport.

THE NEWPORT PICTORIAL.
Official Portraits.

Breconshire in Parliament from 1858 to 1875. His lordship is the Master of the the Tredegar Hunt, and the owner of large estates in the counties of Glamorgan, Brecon and Monmouth. He has always shown great interest in all matters pertaining to Welsh industry and agriculture. He succeeded to the title in 1875, and was created a Viscount December 1905. We are indebted to his lordship for permission to present the series of views of Tredegar House.

TREDEGAR HOUSE (FRONT VIEW). Photo, Mr. C. Gee.

THE LORD LIEUTENANT OF MONMOUTHSHIRE.
(VISCOUNT TREDEGAR).

THE Right Honourable the VISCOUNT TREDEGAR, whose seat is Tredegar Park, Newport, is the Lord Lieutenant of Monmouthshire and Deputy Lieutenant of Breconshire. Viscount Tredegar is the second baron, and was formerly in the 17th Lancers, with whom he took part in the memorable charge at Balaclava. He retired from the army in 1885, since which time he has been Hon. Colonel of the Royal Monmouth Engineer Militia. He represented

GWERN-Y-CLEPPA CROMLECH. Photo, A. & G. Taylor, Newport.

TREDEGAR HOUSE (SIDE VIEW)

DOORWAY, TREDEGAR HOUSE (SIDE ENTRANCE).

THE STABLES, TREDEGAR HOUSE.

Photos, Mr. C. Gee.

DOORWAY, TREDEGAR HOUSE.
(FRONT ENTRANCE).

THE MAYOR OF NEWPORT (COUNCILLOR J. LISCOMBE).

THE TOWN CLERK OF NEWPORT (MR. ALBERT A. NEWMAN).

COUNCILLOR JOHN LISCOMBE was born at Dulverton, Somerset, and is descended from an old family of tanners and leather merchants. He came to Newport in 1872. Councillor Liscombe was returned to Newport Town Council for the old North Ward, on a vacancy, in November, 1892, and since the re-arrangement of the wards has represented the St. Woollos Ward. He is a member of various important committees of the Corporation, including the Education Committee. He has always taken a keen interest in technical education, and for several years was Vice-Chairman of the old Technical Committee. He is now Vice-Chairman of the Lunacy Visiting Committee. In politics, Mr. Liscombe is a Liberal. Not the least memorable feature of Councillor Liscombe's mayoralty will be the opening of the Transporter Bridge, probably about next Easter.

MR. ALBERT A. NEWMAN was born at Newport, and educated at Gloucester and Westminster. Was admitted a Solicitor in 1877. After two years' experience in Lancashire, was appointed Deputy Town Clerk of Newport in 1880, and Town Clerk in 1882. He has thus been the legal adviser of the Corporation during Newport's rapid municipal development of the last quarter of a century. He is also the Clerk of the Urban and Port Sanitary Authorities, the Burial Board, the Lunacy Visiting Committee, and the Education Committee. Besides being a civic official, Mr. Newman has been a citizen soldier, having put in 21 years' service as a Volunteer officer, retiring a short time ago.

A Notable Newport Invention.

RESIDENTS in Newport are rightly credited with being genuine lovers of music and things musical, and for that reason, if for no other, we feel that they will take more than a passing interest in what is being done by one of their number in regard to improving the tone of the piano. As yet little attention has been given locally to the invention of Mr. Hutchinson, though there seems no doubt that it is one fraught with far-reaching consequences. The magnitude of the task before the inventor cannot be over-estimated. The prejudices of opposing interests confront him. His only incentive to press forward comes from an unshakeable confidence in the excellence of that which is the outcome of his own genius and handiwork. It is common knowledge that all efforts to leave the beaten tracks of custom and long usage have generally been so menaced. Convinced as we are that the man and his mission form a noteworthy incident in local life, we have the greatest pleasure in presenting to our readers some particulars and illustrations of Mr. Hutchinson's invention. This gentleman is naturally proud of his achievement, while his frankness and practical demonstrations of the superior tone of his instruments are convincing. In talking with him we gathered that he set out to produce a perfect toned piano, and in his invention of "The Invisible Iron Frame" he claims to have accomplished his object. The public generally can judge of its justness by a visit to his show rooms, where intruments constructed on the new principle may be tested and compared with those of other makers. We venture to say that a visit will be interesting.

As to the invention itself, we will let the inventor put the case in his own words:

"Is the Iron Framed Piano (he asks) of the present day as good and even in tone as the piano made before the iron frame was introduced?

It is admitted that the iron frame is a necessary feature in order to get the required strength put upon the back, as nearly all pianos are now full trichord instead of bichord, but this design and position upsets all possibilities of getting a perfect scale, also bridges on the sounding board.

To use an ordinary iron frame in front of the sounding board, it will be observed that there are two middle bars, which are placed in a highly disadvantageous position, as

they necessitate the bridge being divided into three sections. Hence the bearing of the strings on the sounding board bridge (where the bars cross) is in consequence less effective and the tone of these strings is impoverished and shortened in duration. Unfortunately the mischief does not end here, for the stringing scale has to be tampered with.

In the art of String Scaling, each note should be in correct relative proportion as to distances, length, and weight of string graduated, which will produce tone of an equal musical quality, provided the sounding board is properly constructed. For example, take the Harp, with as perfect a scale as science can make it. The same principle applies to the Piano, as these instruments are similar to each other as far as string scaling is concerned."

To produce the perfect-toned piano on the lines indicated, Mr. Hutchinson has given a considerable amount of time, besides money on patents, and the necessary making of patterns. He is the holder of five patents, all in connection with the one object, viz.: to get an Iron Frame so designed as to receive a free sounding board, one continuous bridge, "no breaks," and a perfect scale.

Had it not been for his practical knowledge of Piano making, with the complications that stood in his way, we fear he could not have succeeded, but by reason of his perseverance and unwavering confidence in the ultimate success of his invention, Mr. Hutchinson has overcome many obstacles and been enabled to bring out a frame, which will be known by the name "Invisible," fixed behind the sounding board.

The tone of the instruments so constructed is beautiful, the materials and workmanship of the best.

The first instrument was made by Messrs. John Brinsmead & Sons, they also made the stringing scale, which is a guarantee for its being correct. This Piano was exhibited at the Trades Exhibition, held in London last year, and was sold at a good price. The criticisms in the "Musical Trades Journal" were as follows:—

Stand No. 83, T. H. Hutchinson, of Newport, Mon. On this stand we found a pianoforte constructed on Mr. Hutchinson's Patent lines of construction, containing what he terms, 'The Invisible Iron Frame.' We quite endorse the idea of making a piano and not cutting the bridge or dividing the strings with a big space, and we are bound to state that none of the objections are to be found in its register, a perfect bridge commencing at the bass, with a round tone, and tapering up to the treble end."

MR. T. H. HUTCHINSON.

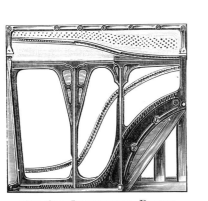

THE OLD INTERRUPTED BRIDGE.

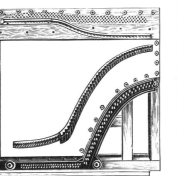

THE "INVISIBLE" FRAME.

THE NEW CONTINUOUS BRIDGE.

ROYAL WORCESTER
Kid-Fitting AMERICAN CORSETS
BRING LUXURIOUS EASE TO THE WEARER.

Above Favourite Model, Princess Hip, 3 Qualities,

16/11 to 21/-

Write for Album of Styles, being a Guide to the Selection of Corsets.

It is the Key of Success to smartness of Dress.

Ask for Name and Address of nearest Agent.

ROYAL WORCESTER CORSETS

The Judgment of PARIS

The above picture represents the judgment of Paris, according premier position to **ROYAL WORCESTER** Kid-fitting American Corsets, casting the old types entirely in the shade.   **PRICE 10/11**

As above Sketch, showing Extreme Princess Hip, 3 Qualities,

21/- to 29/6

ROYAL WORCESTER TRADING Co., . .

20 BLOOMSBURY STREET, LONDON, W.C.

CAERLEON IN 1793.

CHRISTCHURCH, NEAR CAERLEON, SHOWING OLD VICARAGE.

CAERLEON.

One of the most notable places near Newport is CAERLEON, which can be easily reached by road or rail. It is on the Usk, and various explanations have been given for its designation. The most generally favoured one is that which derives it from the old British, Caerllion, the "City of the floods, or waters," evidently in connection with its position on the river Usk, for as viewed from one of the near heights, the meanderings of the river and of its small tributaries in the valley give the city the appearance of being nearly surrounded by water.

Antoninus, in his Itinerary, designates it Isca Legionis Secunda Augusta (Isca being

LLANTARNAM CHURCH.

CHRISTCHURCH, NEAR CAERLEON.

Photos by A. & G. Taylor, Newport.

Usk Latinised). It was also anciently termed Isca Silurum (from the British tribe of the Silures* settled in that district of Monmouthshire). It was also known as Isca Colonæi. It is also thought to have derived its name from Caer Legionis, "City of the Legion," from being, as noted by Antoninus (see above), the head-quarters of the Second Augustan Legion for a long while, until its final withdrawal about A.D. 408.

There is no reason to doubt that the City of the floods, or of the Second Legion, was in the Roman period a place of great importance and of vast strength. Geoffrey of Monmouth (followed in this by Giraldus Cambrensis), gives a description which even if in part extravagant, indicates that it was the seat not only of Roman military power, but of Roman opulence and splendour.

Remains have from time to time been found which support the statements mentioned, and the Caerleon Museum is rich in such.

It was regarded as the metropolitan see of the old British Church, and its Archbishop formed one of the three British Bishops at the Council of Arles in A.D. 315, nearly 300 years before Augustine landed in the Isle of Thanet.

At Caerleon the great British King Arthur held his Court, the deeds of whom and of his "Knights of the Round Table" are recorded in story and in song.

To moderns, Caerleon must always have a deep interest from the fact that here the great poet Tennyson wrote part at least of his "Idylls of the King." He took up his quarters at the old Hanbury Arms Inn, where still remains the room which the poet laureate occupied, while studying the scenes of the Arthurian legend. Writing thence on September 16, 1856, he said: "The Usk murmurs by the windows, and I sit like King Arthur in Caerleon. This is a most quaint half ruined village, of about 1,500 inhabitants, with a little museum of Roman tombstones and other things."

It is difficult now to realise that Caerleon was once an important and proud city. Yet it will well repay examination, and there are remains which afford room for the widest antiquarian speculations. The so-called

THE VILLAGE, CAERLEON.
Photo by A. & G. Taylor, Newport.

*The name is now used by geologists to distinguish the large division of Palæozoic rocks between the old Red Sandstone and the Cambrian Strata—so the Silurian formation !

PARKFIELD PLACE, CLYTHA PARK.

"King Arthur's Round Table" (a circular spot), and the large artificial mound in the Castle are among the objects of chief interest. The village, known as Caerleon Ultra Pontem by the Romans, is on the side of the river opposite to that occupied by the town. Our illustrations sufficiently indicate the existing main features, both of Caerleon and of the Village "Ultra Pontem."

STOW PARK CRESCENT. Photos by A. & G. Taylor, Newport.

St. Julian's.

From Caerleon, a walk leads through hanging woods and over fertile meadows to St. Julian's, a place, says Coxe, in his "History of Monmouthshire," once remarkable for the residence of the celebrated Lord Herbert of Cherbury;* it is situated nearly mid-way between Caerleon and Newport, on the banks of the Usk. "The building, now converted into a farm house, has been lately much reduced from its original size; part of the south front has been modernised, part remains in its former state; and the whole presents a motley combination, which, at the same expense, might have preserved the venerable appearance of the old mansion, and the comforts of a modern house. The ancient Gothic porch, which still forms the entrance, is likely to be soon destroyed, according to the plans adopted in the present alterations. The north front which has been permitted to retain its antique appearance is a picturesque object, backed by a wooded eminence, and overhanging the abrupt banks of the Usk.

"The inside has some remains of former magnificence, particularly in the staircase, and several Gothic doorways. Two apartments retain their ancient dimensions, but were about to be converted into smaller rooms; the lower apartment was 36 feet in length, 20 broad, and 17 high; the upper 45 by 20, and of the same height; against the walls are the remains of slender pillars of the Gothic style.

*We may add that Edward Herbert, Lord of Cherbury, was born at Montgomery Castle, in 1581. He was made a Knight of the Bath by James I., served with distinction in the Netherlands, was twice Ambassador to France, and on his return, in 1625, was created an Irish Peer (which carried with it a seat in the Irish House of Lords), and afterwards an English Baron. His literary acquirements were great, and among his works may be named a "Life of Henry VIII.," and "De Veritate." During the Civil Wars he joined the Parliamentarians, but afterwards left them, and died in 1648. His brother was the celebrated George Herbert, born 1598, who became eminent as a divine and a poet, dying early in life at his Rectory of Bemerton, Wilts, in 1632. As connected with so distinguished a family, ST. JULIAN'S is of far more than local interest.

"Near the house is an old barn of small dimensions, which was once part of the chapel of St. Julius, from whom the place derived its appellation; on the south wall are the remains of an arched entrance, which is now half filled up; the east and west windows still remain in their original state. According to the ancient tradition, this chapel and mansion were once included within the Town of Caerleon."†

Public Recreation Grounds.

For a long period and until quite a recent date, Newport had only one public recreation ground, namely Park Square, an enclosure useful certainly, and commanding from its higher portion a fine view or two, but entirely too small and out of proportion for the want of a growing town like Newport. It was no doubt in view of this fact that some twelve or thirteen years ago Lord Tredegar very generously presented to the town a splendidly situated piece of land, no less than twenty-three acres in extent, situate on a gently rising site south of the town, and bounded on its upper side by Waterloo Road and on the lower by Cardiff Road, the Belle Vue Road on one side forming it roughly into a triangle. This splendid site, commanding beautiful views and easy of access, Mr. Thos. H. Mawson, of Windermere, was, after a spirited competition, selected and authorised by the Corporation to lay out, which he did in a manner that must satisfy the most fastidious. Besides finely undulating walks and convenient carriage drives, there are pavilion, conservatories, fountains, band stand and terraces. There is also a well fitted playground for children. A small ornamental lake with waterfall, admirably arranged, gives a pleasing variety; and sundry rock-work, rosary, and well-planned shrubberies, form with their accessories a *coup d'œil* which it would be difficult to surpass.

† Caerleon is alluded to as "Caerleon Strong" in Spenser's "Faery Queen," (Canto x., Stanza xxv.)

Our views of this beautiful park, specially selected and taken for the NEWPORT PICTORIAL, serve to give a good idea as to how happily Lord Tredegar's noble gift to the town has been treated, and as to how largely it must in the future increase the amenities and add to the permanent attractions of the town. Second only to Lord Tredegar's generosity is to be reckoned the liberality and public spirit with which the Corporation gave its object full effect in the laying out of the ground.

Almost every kind of shrub suitable for open air and other climate is there to be found. The conservatories are filled with choice flowers, exotics, and sub-tropical plants, and he who cannot here feast upon the beauties of nature and art and be satisfied must indeed be hard to please.

Another Park recently acquired is that of Beechwood, on the Chepstow Road, formerly and up to the time of the Corporation securing it, a private residence. Various alterations have been made in the grounds since that date, but more remains to be done. There is a large bowling green, and seats are abundantly provided. On the edge of the estate, and abutting the public road, is a finely wooded strip known as the Dingle, through which a rivulet flows in the wetter portion of the year. This plantation, of considerable length, is obviously capable of treatment which would render it a striking feature of Beechwood.

The views from this Park and its immediate neighbourhood are as varied as they are impressive.

There is also Shaftesbury Park Recreation Ground, along the banks of the Usk between the river and Crindau Pill, where accommodation is provided for football. hockey and cricket, to which the now popular game of bowls is to be added. It meets a great want of the numerous juvenile population in the district.

WALES V. NEW ZEALAND. Played at Cardiff, and won by Wales by 1 try (3 points) to nil.

The Welsh International Team.

Photo, A. & G. Taylor.

The New Zealand Team.

J. W. Stead.   C. Seeling.   J. O'Sullivan.   D. M'Gregor.   F. Newton.   A. M'Donald.
F. Roberts.   F. Glasgow.   S. Casey.   D. Gallaher.   G. Gillett.   R. G. Deans.   W. J. Wallace.
G. Tyler.   I. Hunter.   H. J. Mynott.   *Photo, A. & G. Taylor.*

Printed & Published by the Proprietor, W. Jones, Cambrian Printing Works. 159 Commercial Street, Newport, Mon.

W. JONES, for Commercial Stationery & all Office Requisites.
.... Account Books to Suit all requirements.
The LEADING HOUSE for LEATHER & FANCY GOODS,
with the Finest and most Comprehensive Collection in the District.

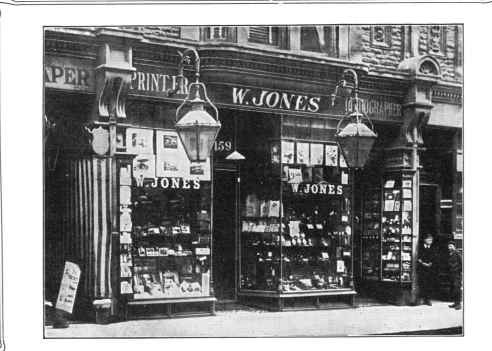

DRESSING CASES.
Ladies' Hand Bags.
Wrist Bags.
Fitted Bags.
Chatelaine Bags.
Gents' Travelling Bags.

PURSES.
A Noted Line.
Every Price and Kind.

Ladies' Companions.
Glove and Handkerchief
Boxes and Cases.
Brush Cases, Ladies' and
Gent's.
Jewel and Trinket Cases.

EBONY GOODS.
A large display of Brushes,
Mirrors, Toilet Requisites,
etc., with Silver Initials
fixed free.

SERVIETTE RINGS,
with Silver Initials, from 1/-
WRITING & BLOTTING Cases.
Pocket Books.
Letts' Cases, &c.

FRAMES
Of all Sizes and Patterns,
in Leather, Brass, Copper
and Mouldings.

POST CARDS.
A Wonderful Collection displayed on Patent Stands.

Fountain & Stylographic
Pens, all the best makes, at
all prices. Special line at 1/-

INKS (all makes) for Copying
and Drawing. Agents for
Chin Chin and Pelican.

PLAYING CARDS & CARD GAMES
in great variety.

BOOKS.
Bibles, Teacher's Editions,
Illustrated, &c.

Prayer & Hymns, in Cases
or separate.

Reward Books, English
Classics, from **6d.**

Leading Novels, from **6d.**

Children's Picture Books
a Speciality.

Birthday Text Books.

The Poets.

Devotional.

ALBUMS.
Photograph.	Post Card.
Autograph.	Scrap.
Stamp.	At Home.
Address.	Recipe.
Confession.	

Artists' Materials
of every description.
Painting Copies let out on hire.
Instrument Cases, Colour Boxes

159 Commercial Street, Newport, Mon.

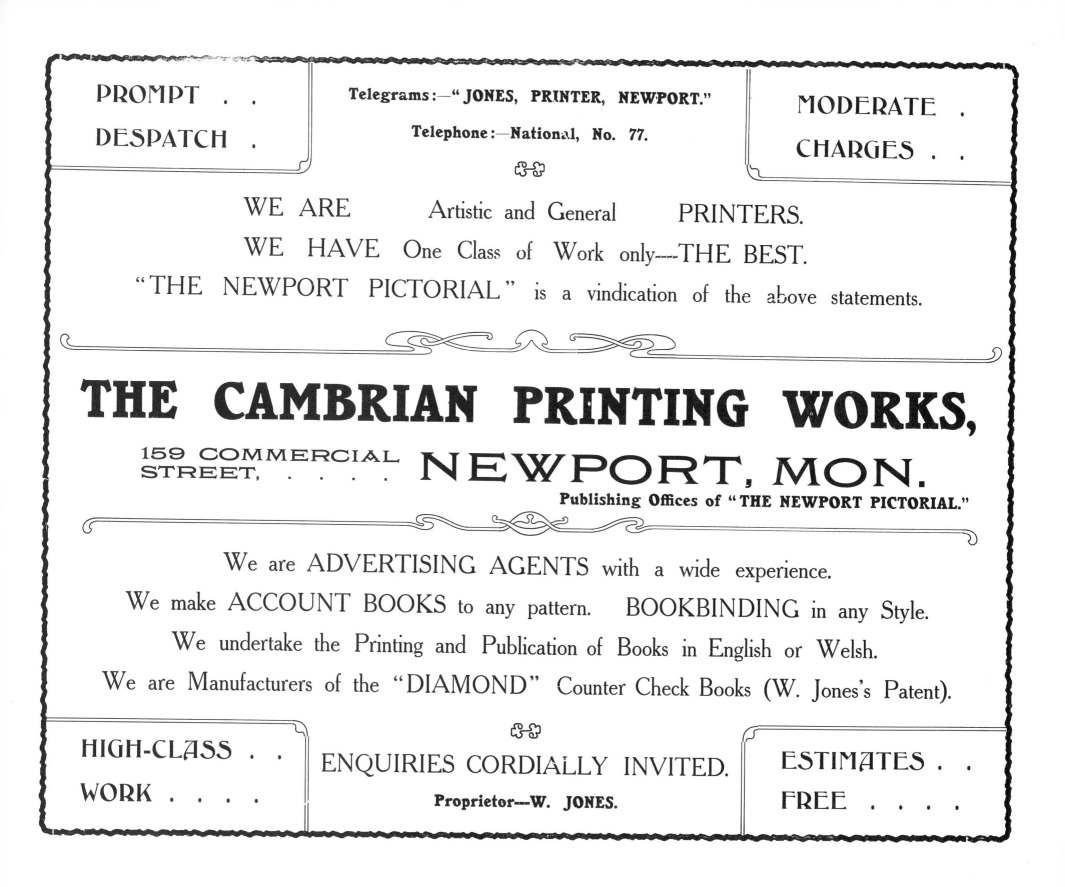

PROMPT . .

DESPATCH .

Telegrams:—"JONES, PRINTER, NEWPORT."

Telephone:—National, No. 77.

MODERATE .

CHARGES . .

WE ARE   Artistic and General   PRINTERS.

WE HAVE One Class of Work only----THE BEST.

"THE NEWPORT PICTORIAL" is a vindication of the above statements.

THE CAMBRIAN PRINTING WORKS,

159 COMMERCIAL STREET, ... NEWPORT, MON.

Publishing Offices of "THE NEWPORT PICTORIAL."

We are ADVERTISING AGENTS with a wide experience.

We make ACCOUNT BOOKS to any pattern.   BOOKBINDING in any Style.

We undertake the Printing and Publication of Books in English or Welsh.

We are Manufacturers of the "DIAMOND" Counter Check Books (W. Jones's Patent).

HIGH-CLASS . .

WORK . . . .

ENQUIRIES CORDIALLY INVITED.

Proprietor---W. JONES.

ESTIMATES . .

FREE . . . .